OCT **1** **7** 2006

OCT **1** **7** 2006

SPORT SHOOTING

RIFLES AND SHOTGUNS

SPORT SHOOTING

RIFLES AND SHOTGUNS

Octavio Díez

Author
Octavio Díez Cámara

Design and Layout
punto5 | Raül González & Eva Snijders

Editorial Co-ordination
E. Marín

English Translation
David Buss

ISBN 84-933924-8-0
Legal Deposit B-183/2006

2006 © Editorial Project
UDYAT SL

Printed in Spain

index

Shooting is continuously making technical advances. The newest weapons are the result of various centuries of continuous evolution.

The history of long arms

In the chapters of this book

the reader will find a wide range of options, models and proposals from the world of long arms, including rifles, shotguns and carbines, representing many different designs, actions and types of ammunition. This wide range of firearms has changed considerably over time and every year new innovations are introduced, both technical and aesthetic. This book includes details and explanations of the different models, ammunition, accessories and sporting disciplines for which the different long arm models have been designed. The wide range of designs, manufacturers and models makes it impossible to include all the weapons available. Therefore, we present the most famous models, companies with an international reputation and the most popular forms of shooting.

The transformation of the rifle

The rifle is the outstanding weapon in its category. It is used by hunters, sportsmen, adventurers, the military, police and other groups. This varied use, together with the changes in society brought about by war and other types of conflict have heavily influenced the development of long arms and given rise to new models.

Changes in design

The rifle has evolved from a single shot model, in which the powder was ignited by a spark or with the help of a wick, to modern semiautomatic models that are able to fire more than one hundred times a minute, limited only by the capacity of the magazine.

These changes, which reached their height during the 20th century, was, of course, influenced greatly by the different wars that occurred, but also by the personal inventiveness of the designers and manufacturers, who developed models which responded to the different needs of the military, hunters, sports shooters, etc. Man has always had to coexist with weapons, but over recent decades, different countries have taken varying views of firearms. Today, the numbers involved in some kind of hunting or sports shooting is estimated to be about five per cent in the United States of America.

A safety located behind the firing pin in a lever action rifle designed for hunting.

Historical evolution

The first references to the rifle go back to the time when powder began to be used to impel projectiles shot by artillery pieces. A similar concept evolved into guns with a long, slim barrel fixed to a piece of wood, with an ignition device located on the side.

The next great advance was the arquebus, which was equipped with a coil of wick to ignite the shot. The wick was eventually replaced by a flint mechanism that caused a spark when it hit a metal pan. These arms were muzzle-loaded by introducing the powder, positioning the projectile, which was initially a round metal shot, and then ramming them both into the deepest part of the bore with a wooden rod.

By the beginning of the 19th century, these weapons had become very accurate, simple and deadly firearms. Due to their high cost and restricted demand, they were mainly confined to the military.

The Anglican clergyman John Forsyth understood that the main problem with flint-lock guns was that they were not reliable in damp weather. He designed a different priming system in which an enclosed charge was ignited by a percussion cap when struck by a hammer.

Fond of game shooting, he realized the major problem with the flint-lock gun was its unreliability in damp conditions. As a consequence of this and other developments, breech-loaded models were developed, facilitating the action and reducing the reloading time. There were also adaptations in which the bore included grooves known as rifling that gave the projectile a spinning movement on its passage through the barrel and increasing muzzle speed and accuracy.

Progressive changes

Further developments included the appearance of the so-called "fusiles de chasses" made at the Imperial Arsenal in Tulle, France, which improved the sights by adopting a leaf sight that moved according to the distance of the target.

Another substantial modification implied enclosing the powder and the projectile with paper, thereby reducing the reloading time. These improvements were included in the Sharps 1853 and the Spencer carbine.

A still-more important step was the appearance of the metallic cartridge, including the powder, the projectile and the ignition in the same package. This led to faster loading weapons and the appearance of the first European bolt action models and lever actions such as the Swiss Martini system or American lever action weapons.

It was the German gunsmith, Peter Paul Mauser, who, in 1865, perfected the manual action that allowed the sequential feeding of cartridges, with a safety for blocking the firing system. After this, there were rapid increases in firing speed and accuracy. These changes were, of course avidly followed by the military, as even small changes in weaponry could lead to the difference between victory or defeat in battle.

Cartridges with bronze projectiles such as the 1886 Lebel were developed and vertical magazines or clips such as the one invented by the Austrian, Ferdinand von Mannlicher were adopted to avoid the accidents which often occurred when tubular magazines housing tipped projectiles were used.

The 20th Century

At the beginning of the last century, other bolt action weapons, such as the American Krag-Jorgensen and Springfield, the Russian Mosin-Nagant, the Japanese Arisaka or the Italian Carcano became popular. At the same time, new semiautomatic models were developed based on designs such as the Italian Cei-Rigotti of 1900 or the Mexican Mondragón of 1907.

Rapid development

The First and Second World Wars initiated a period of rapid developments in rifle technology. In fact, the hundreds of thousands of deaths which occurred among infantrymen in the trenches during battles such as Ypres and the Somme were largely due to the development of rifle technology.

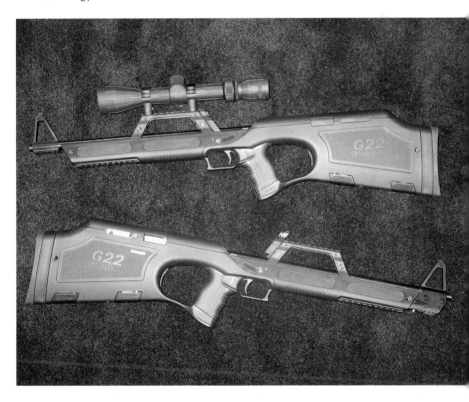

These developments were later incorporated into models for civilians. Among the improvements introduced by the military were magazines with a greater capacity, the introduction of gas exhaust holes in the actions to make automatic firing easier and more sophisticated sights.

The 21st century is on the brink of revolutionary technical advances. The design and materials of weapons such as this G22 Walther carbine are constantly being improved.

I : 10

Detail of a spark key. The gun was ignited by the spark from the flint igniting the powder.

The history of long arms has seen many different firing systems including this percussion ignition model.

Perhaps the most important changes were the introduction of new and different types of ammunition, resulting in longer ranges and multipurpose models. Ammunition manufacturers have played an important role in the development of firearms, as the use of a particular type of ammunition can have a spectacular effect on performance.

Research has led to developments such as caseless ammunition, electronic ignition systems or barrels coated with graphite and other substances, although some of

these experiments have had very limited success due to technical problems. Other developments, such as barrels tempered by cryogenic treatment, or stocks designed with lighter, more ergonomic synthetic materials, have been successfully introduced. Most modern models use technical improvements that improve performance to a degree that would have been unthinkable a century ago.

Carbines

"A firearm composed off the same pieces as the rifle, but shorter" is one of the many definitions of "carbine" that can be found in dictionaries and encyclopedias. In effect, the carbine is a type of long arm which is shorter than a rifle, basically to make it easier to carry on the battlefield. They were developed to equip the cavalry and other types of military with a type of weapon they needed.

Over time, the arms known as carbines have also been adopted by civil users, both in manual and semiautomatic forms. The reality is that today there is no real definition of the size of a carbine or a rifle and the designation owes more to commercial and even legal criteria. For example, a manufacturer may call the short version of a rifle a carbine, even though it may be the same length as the rifle made by another manufacturer, as, for example, the Winchester lever action rifles which are quite short.

More recently, weapons have been designated as carbines according to the caliber. Firearms designed to use the popular .22 Long rifle (LR), and similar cartridges such as the 22 Winchester Magnum, are called carbines, more for their lack of fire power and than because of their overall length. The term carbine is now used for many sport shooting models.

Even some weapons originally used by the police or military have become known as carbines. Various types of assault rifles and sub-machine guns equipped with semiautomatic actions and other smaller changes to make them suitable for the civil market and adapted to the normal caliber of short arms, such as the 9x19 mm Parabellum, the .45 ACP and others are called carbines.

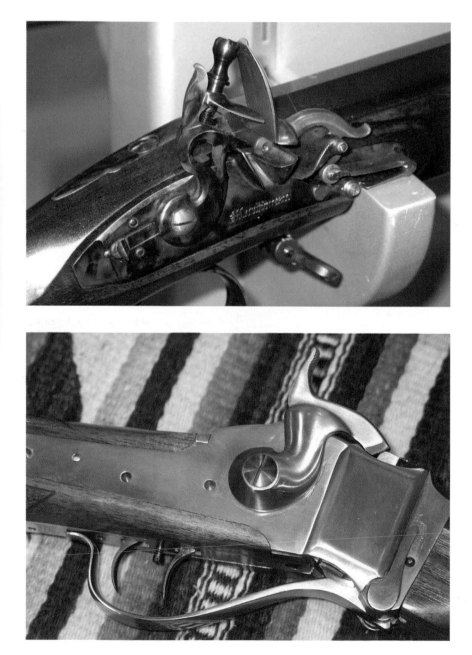

Shotguns

In the USA, a shotgun is defined as "a weapon designed or redesigned, made or remade, and intended to be fired from the shoulder, and designed and redesigned and made or remade to use the energy of the explosive in a fixed shotgun shell to fire through a smooth bore either a number of ball shot or a single projectile for each single pull of the trigger". There are many varieties of shotgun – side-by-side, over-and-under or single barrel – using manual, pump or semiautomatic actions. The first shotguns began to appear in the 18th century and followed a classic side-by-side design, although there were also single-barreled models.

eventually the center fire shells used today were developed. In the early period, shells were made of paper or cardboard. Today, plastic materials are used. The next developments were heavily influenced by one man, John Browning, who was born in 1855 in Ogden, Utah. By his death in 1926, he held over a hundred patents for guns, including machine-guns, rifles and both semi-automatic and pump action shotguns, which were used by the US Army.

A later development were under-and-over shotguns, with, as the name suggests, one barrel superposed

Advances in the design and manufacture of long arms in recent decades has improved performance substantially.

These shotguns were made to shoot shells in which the main charge was small lead pellets designed to shoot down birds and small animals. They were equipped with exterior firing pins which were cocked manually.

The first shells were not very reliable and often blew up in the face of the user. The first great advance was introduced by the Parisian gunsmith, Casimir Lefaucheux, who positioned a vertical firing pin on the side. This, how ever, still led to problem and

over the other. Other innovations developments included the use of aluminum and other lightweight materials instead of steel for the action mechanism and synthetic materials for trigger guards and stocks. This continuous technological progress has transformed shotguns, even though its use remains basically unchanged.

Today, there is a wide range of shotguns available, from the prohibitively expensive to cheap, mass-produced models, and they are sold by the million.

A close up of the pistol grip of a bolt action rifle, with fine nonslip checkering making it easier to hold the weapon.

Bolt action rifles

In the many decades

that bolt action rifles have been in military use they have acquired a reputation for reliability, simplicity, robustness and accuracy. Because of those qualities, increasing numbers of hunters and sport shooters are choosing this option. The arms industry has welcomed the popularity of this type of weapon by designing and manufacturing a new generation of bolt action weapons with details such as glass fiber stocks, graphite barrels, electronic ignition systems or adjustable triggers.

I : 14

The action

The bolt action is the most significant element of this type of weapon. The characteristics of the action usually define the basic form of the rifle, although both the design and elements such as the barrel, stock or sights vary. The action can also vary according to the type of cartridge for which it is designed.

Specific configurations

Most bolt action rifles are bought by hunters of various types.

The first long arms with a bolt action were introduced at the end of the 19th century. Since then, the basic action has constantly evolved to adapt to the conditions of each era and to the needs of users.

Basically, the bolt action is a manual device whereby the shooter, using a linear or rotary movement, introduces a cartridge from the magazine into the breech, and extracts the empty cartridge case automatically by making the opposite movement.

A lot of rifles and some shotguns use a bolt action. The bolt is in fact a cylindrical rod that is situated behind the firing chamber. It usually has twin tabs that project into channels in the frame of the gun, which turn into cuts on the sides of the main channels, locking the bolt into position when the bolt closes behind the cartridge in the breech. The bolt propels the cartridge into the chamber and then turns to lock in place. By this action, the breech is totally enclosed except for the bore of the barrel. After firing, the empty cartridge case is ejected by turning the bolt back and pulling it rearwards. The bolt is moved in and out by the bolt handle. The bolt action itself is usually some type of cylinder made of very robust materials, generally steel. It must be very resistant, because it will have to absorb part of the energy generated by firing, and bolt actions are notable for the resistance they offer against the pressures generated by the most powerful cartridges.

Bolt action details

A hooked device known as the extractor hook pulls the case out of the chamber as the breech mechanism is opened. In bolt action rifles, the extractor hook brings the cartridge case to the ejector which then takes over and tosses the case from the gun. In guns with manual actions, such as the bolt action, safeties are essential. The safety on a model like, for example the Ruger Mark II, blocks both the trigger and the striker and the shooter can see that the safety is engaged. However, in the middle position, the bolt can be turned while the trigger is still blocked.

Many bolt action rifles, such as the Model 70 Winchester, also have holes in the bolt which allows venting of the high pressure gases generated by firing to be dissipated. The action of the rifle varies in length, from short to long, depending on the type of cartridge for which it is designed.

Bolt action weapons

Most bolt action rifles are produced either in Europe or in the United States, where numerous companies promote all types of models and variants. Hunters and sport shooters require a different model of rifle although both types share more and more general details.

European bolt action rifles

Many European companies manufacture bolt action rifles. The Austrian company, Steyr Mannlicher, has some quite novel concepts that include the Scout model, whose general design was thought out by the American, Jeff Cooper. It is a weapon with a very modern design and is made with effectiveness, accuracy and lightness in mind. It includes the possibility of storing a spare magazine, a cold forged barrel and a light composite stock. The weapon is further lightened by the exterior grooving of the barrel.

Steyr Mannlicher also manufactures models based on the Mannlicher 96, such as the Classic and the more recent Extreme Light and Jagdmatch. The Classic models are available with a normal or extended Goiserer-type stock.

Both have the same length and barrel. The most recent light version only weighs 2.7 kg for easier carrying but is

Browning produces excellent hunting rifles in Belgium and the United States that sell well in many markets.

I : 16

This weapon is equipped with a safety lever with three positions, sited behind the bolt.

only available in low or medium calibers. The Steyr Elite and SSG 04 lines are very recent. The SSG 04 has a muzzle brake fixed to its barrel and the magazine can hold ten .308 or .300 Winchester Magnum cartridges.

The normal version costs about 2,580 euros, and the compact variant, with a barrel varying in length from 51 to 60 centimeters, costs 2,388 euros. Sako is a Finnish gunmaker that produces very high quality products.

Bolt action rifles are very accurate and are widely used and trusted by hunters.

The 75 model is destined for hunting and includes variants such as the Hunter, Deluxe or Finnlight that have different finishes and use different materials for the stocks.

Models such as the 75 Varmint, with a fine stock of laminated wood and a heavy barrel that can be chambered for calibers like the 6 mm PPC or the .22-250 are more suitable for precision shooting.

The TRG 22 and 42 are more elaborate bolt action weapons with such precision engineering and great accuracy that they have been selected by some elite police groups for their snipers.

These arms have an extraordinarily ergonomic stock, a carefully manufactured action and an excellent barrel. The TRG 22 can be equipped with a UIT-standard diopter.

robust linear action The different series include the Standard, Prestige, Luxus, Grand Luxe and Super Luxus Exklusiv, Super Exklusiv and Royal series with many options of finish and chasing.

The cheapest weapon costs a little over two thousand euros while the most expensive may exceed sixteen thousand euros. These prices give a good idea of the quality of these firearms.

Sauer is a German company with a long history and great experience in producing weapons. The present offer concentrates mainly on the 90, 92 and 202 models.

The Winchester 70 Classic model is an accurate, well-made and comparatively cheap weapon with many options and sells well.

Central European models

In Germany, the Czech Republic and other nations in Central Europe, there are a large number of gun lovers and hunters practicing different types of shooting. Because of the large market, there are many companies manufacturing all types of long arms, generally weapons with a superior finish and good performance.

The models of the German company, Blazer, are centered on the R93 model, which includes an accurate,

The Model 202 includes variants such as the Elegance, which includes details such as beautiful wooden stock, and a mechanism with a satin finish; the Forest, which has a detachable magazine for five cartridges; or the Outback, which is characterized by its light, black, synthetic stock.

A special variant of the Model 202 is the Take Down, which can be broken down into two parts for easier carrying. It is an extremely robustly designed weapon which is aimed at hunters and fires powerful cartridges such as the .375 Holland & Holland and the .416 Remington Magnum.

Mauser is also of German origin, although some manufacturing is now carried out in other countries. The most recent range is based on the M03 rifle, which has variants with fine engravings on the action. The M03 is distinguished by its safety lever, which has two positions and is located on the rear of the bolt. This is a very handy position for activating and deactivating it with the thumb, without losing sight of the prey.

American leadership

The large manufacturers of the United States maintain a classic line that has evolved with respect to performance, details and operation.

Remington centers its recent offers on the Seven, 673, 710 and 700 models. The 700 is the range with the greatest number of variants, as the basic model has given rise to many different options that fire metal cartridges and even a few muzzle-loading models.

The ADL and BDL series are some of the most widely used hunting models, since they include mechanical sights that do not require viewfinders.

More elaborate and accurate are options like the LSS or VS SF. The LSS has a laminated stock and chromed 24" or 26" barrel and the VS SF has a carbon fiber synthetic stock and a heavy 26" barrel that is available in the regular version or with exterior grooving.

Currently, the Remington 700 series has more than forty options, not including those chambered to hold up to twenty-four cartridges of different characteristics, a combination that leads to hundreds of different offers.

Winchester weapons also sell really well. They are centered on another classic, the Model 70. To update the model, arms that are adapted to new cartridges such as the .25 Winchester Short Magnum have been produced, while classic, versatile options such as the .270 Winchester or .300 Winchester Magnum remain popular.

To bring their range up to date, Winchester have worked on details such as stocks with non-slip properties or camouflage finishes. Among the most recent models are the Ultimate Shadow, Sporter LT, Stealth II and the Coyote, whose multitude of features means it can be used for precision shooting or for hunting big game.

Browning continues to concentrate its offer on the accurate A-Bolt, a range with more than a hundred different variants. The most recent models are the M-1000 Eclipse, with a thumbhole type stock and the Mountain Ti, which includes a titanium locking action and a syn-

The locking action of this type of long arms is usually made from a steel block to make it as strong as possible.

Today's market offers many type of bolt action guns produced by different manufacturers.

Detail of the design of the bolt action, which is a mechanical action that blocks the chamber and activates ignition of the cartridge.

The action of these rifles allows the shooter to load and unload manually. It is simple to use and very reliable.

thetic stock that reduces the weight to a little less than two and a half kilograms.

Another great American manufacturer is Weatherby. This company has a range of arms with an excellent finish and is described by many as the manufacturer of the best factory-made trigger.

These qualities guarantee a maximum accuracy of less than ½ MOA at one hundred meters with standard ammunition in all their products. Rifles such as the DRG, TRR Magnum or Safari Custom, which are constructed around the solid Mark V action, a system in which the bolt movement only requires a turn of 54°, are especially robust.

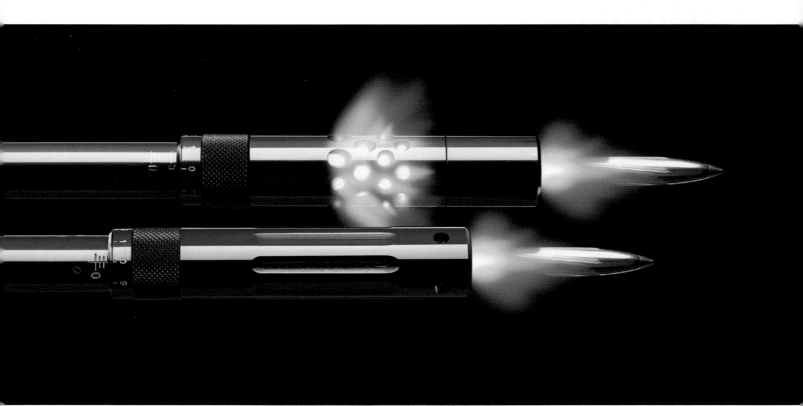

Some semiautomatic rifles have details such as a BOSS (ballistic optimizing shooting system) which reduces recoil and improves accuracy.

Semiautomatic Rifles

Semiautomatic rifles

enjoy popularity among gun lovers as they can rapidly fire various shots consecutively without reloading. This type of action allows up to six consecutive shots within a few seconds. In many countries, the use of these weapons by civilians is prohibited due to their excessive firepower, and there are restrictions on the type of cartridges that can be used. Semiautomatic rifles are used in hunting to give extra capacity to bring down an animal that is wounded or difficult to hit. However, to increase the chances of survival of the animal, there are limitations on the maximum number of cartridges that can be loaded in a gun while hunting. Semiautomatics are also widely used by sport shooters, where the legal limitations are not so great, although their use is still restricted. For example, until repealed by the current Bush administration in 2004, the sale of arms with magazines that have a capacity of over ten cartridges was prohibited in the United States. The speed and sequence of firing, their simplicity of use, the magazines and the design are just some of the elements that attract potential users, especially informal shooters.

A different concept

In general, with some design differences, the characteristic shape and makeup of semiautomatic rifles is very similar to that of bolt action rifles, as is the ammunition they use, although the action of the semiautomatic rifle is normally not adapted to shoot the powerful African cartridges. However, there are exceptions, and more and more models are being adapted for the powerful .50 Browning cartridge that is becoming popular for hunting prey located at a range of more than a kilometer.

The biggest difference between semiautomatic and bolt action rifles is that semiautomatics, like bolt actions, shoot one cartridge every time the trigger is pulled, but use the energy generated by firing to eject the empty cartridge case and insert the next cartridge into the chamber of the firearm. Due to this automatic process, the shooter can concentrate on observing and aiming at the prey.

A century of history

Semiautomatic weapons were developed to satisfy the needs of the military and police, who were the first groups to use these weapons. In 1905, a Winchester rifle was put on sale that incorporated a simple inertia recovery action and shot .35 WSL (Winchester Self Loading) cartridges, low power ammunition that was not very useful for hunting. A short time later, this rifle was adapted to shoot .351 WSL and .401 SWL cartridges, which had more power as they

The Italian company, Benelli manufactures a well-designed semiautomatic rifle that performs impressively.

could include expansive bullets. Following the trend, Remington developed, in 1906, its Model 8, a weapon that is considered by some enthusiasts as the first semiautomatic weapon with a true sports application. Its most characteristic element was a spring on the exterior of the barrel to guarantee the consecutive firing of .35 Remington ammunition. Although the cartridges were not really suitable for hunting, the model was manufactured until 1950 due to its good design and its accuracy.

Military models

During World War II, numerous types of automatic or semiautomatic rifles were manufactured which, when the war finished, became surplus to requirements. Part of this surplus, such as many examples of the M1 Garand, found its way onto the civilian market. They were well received because they were, and still are, sold at a low price and because their .30-06 Springfield cartridges could be used to bring down all types of big game.

In recent decades, numerous semiautomatic models have been developed in Europe, including this rifle made by Heckler und Koch.

The SL-81 is a semiautomatic rifle whose design is based on the most recent military technology. It was conceived for the civilian market and is particularly popular among sport shooters.

The acceptance of the Garand and its successors, the M1A and M14, among gun lovers both in the United States and other countries was not only centered on these models. With the introduction of its successor, the now mythical M16, there was a demand for civilian variants adapted to semiautomatic shooting, leading to the birth of the AR-15. This is a light weapon of which hundreds of thousands have been sold all over the world, with the number of variants continuing to grow and the performance improving with new innovations.

Different mechanical types

A characteristic semiautomatic magazine used in various firearms.

Over recent decades, different semiautomatic concepts have been developed. Some rifles, such as the historic Heckler und Koch H&K 940/941 used a system with a semi-rigid locking action with rollers similar to those developed by the German technicians who helped to conceive the CEMTE assault rifle.

This system obliges the shooter to use considerable force on the lever assembly – located on the right side – to move the locking action backwards and to release the rollers of the locking action, which close the chamber independently of the pressure exerted by the recoil spring. Its backward and forward movement is rather violent and produces a characteristic noise, although it has the advantage that during rapid firing there is almost no deviation of the aim.

Another type of action was that developed by the Belgian company, Browning International. The body of the locking action is provided with a movable metal cover that prevents dirt entering. These guns use a unique, self-regulating gas system. If the load is light, the majority of the energy of the expanding gases is recycled to operate the action, while with larger loads the excess gas is expelled through the lateral vents in the piston, thereby reducing recoil considerably.

Current models

The catalogues of the bigger manufacturers include various examples of semiautomatic models, whose finish and performance are constantly improving. This constant renewal, their acceptance among hunters, their remarkable reliability and accuracy and the fact that they are more versatile than lever action rifles make them popular weapons.

New models

One of the most recent offers is the Model SBL 2000 made by the German company, Heckler und Koch. It was developed for hunters and its qualities include a cold-steel floating barrel that offers good accuracy, fixed front sights and mounts for a viewfinder, hand guards and a non-slip stock. It can use magazines for 2, 5 or 10 cartridges. Heckler und Koch offer variants that are adapted for ammunition such as the .308 and .30-06 and there is even a Light version modified to a length of 105 cm and a weight of 3.3 kg to make it more manageable. Until recently, H&K also offered the SL6 and SL7. These semiautomatic weapons have an inertia locking action noted for its reliability in the worst conditions.

The 630 and 940/941 models are aimed more at sport shooting, although their general conception is similar. The Model 630 is available in a version adapted to the .222 Remington for sale in countries where NATO .223

ammunition is prohibited, whereas the Model 940/941 can be adapted to powerful cartridges such as the 7x64 mm. Both weapons have magazines with a capacity of up to ten cartridges.

The Sl8-1 offers a more futuristic aspect. It is a sporting adaptation that evolved from the G36 assault rifle, with details conceived for sport shooting. The cheekpiece, extended rear sight and extensive use of synthetic materials are some of the notable features of the S18-1.

Browning

Another model that has been widely used by hunters since its introduction in 1967 is the Browning BAR.

The basic rifle has evolved into the present Short Trac and Long Trac series.

Several countries manufacture rifles based on the Dragunov, a very accurate semiautomatic rifle with a flowing line and many fine details.

Semiautomatic rifles have actions that load new cartridges in the chamber and automatically eject the empty cartridge cases.

The popularity of semiautomatic rifles was initially based on the sale of military weapons like this Garand, which are still highly popular.

The Short Trac is adapted for cartridges such as the .243 Winchester and .308 and has a shorter mechanism. The Long Trac is available in variants which fire the powerful 7 mm Remington Magnum and .300 Winchester Magnum. Both ranges are characterized by their aluminum action case and forged steel barrel, a combination that offers lightness and accuracy.

Other variants of the BAR series include the Lightweight Stalker designed for better handling and resistance and the Safari, an optimal hunting weapon, which is available with the BOSS (Ballistic Optimizing Shooting System) system, which consists of a compensator fixed to the muzzle to improve grouping.

Remington

Remington is the only major American company that includes semi-automatic rifles in its present line. Remington's main model is the 7400 which uses a gas-propelled action and has a rotary locking action that offers very robust locking.

The present options include the Synthetic, Carbine and Weathermaster models, which are available in satin, mat black, or chrome mat finish. The length varies, since the rifles can be fitted with an 18.5" or 21" barrel. The magazine can store four cartridges, with a fifth in the chamber.

Ruger

Ruger continues to develop new options based on its Mini-14 design, which is appreciated by both hunters and sport shooters. The basic model, which dates from 1975, has been followed by others, including the current Mini Ranch series.

Other models

The Finnish company, Valmet, produces the Hunter rifle, which is based on a Kalashnikov-type action adapted to the characteristic harsh conditions of the country. Its automatic action and elegant lines allow fast shooting sequences and offer more than acceptable accuracy and power.

Browning, which manufactures guns in Belgium and the USA, leads the market in semiautomatic arms for hunters.

Benelli manufactures the Argon, a semiautomatic rifle with a cryogenically treated barrel and chamber to improve accuracy.

The distinctive advanced rear sight, designed to facilitate more instinctive and rapid aiming is a notable feature of this weapon.

The Russia market offers various options based mainly on semiautomatic designs that have proved their efficiency in military circles.

The Vyatskie Polyany Machine Building Plant, known commercially as Molot, manufacture the Vepr model, of which several options are available.

One of the best is the Vepr Super model, which has a special 55 cm barrel. It incorporates an adjustable rear sight to shoot at ranges of between 100 and 300 meters and includes a mount to fix a viewfinder. Its semiautomatic system includes a locking action with three lugs.

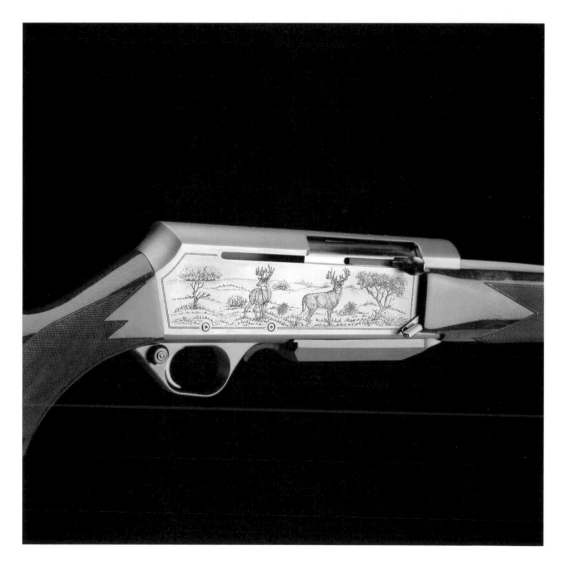

Shooting tables allow the shooter to support the weapon and avoid vibration.

Bench Rest Shooting

Bench Rest

is a type of high-precision rifle shooting that is becoming more and more popular among sportsmen. The objective is to obtain the most closed groupings using various shots. This demands extremely proficient shooting and weapons, and accessories designed and manufactured to obtain the highest level of performance. Both sport shooters who want to improve their skills to participate in long arms shooting competitions and hunters seeking improvements in their hunting techniques are great enthusiasts of Bench Rest shooting.

I : 30

The history of Bench Rest

The discipline of Bench Rest shooting is relatively young, although there are references to shooting competitions organized in the United States in the 17th and 18th centuries to find out who the best gunman of the area was. At that time, the target had a clear marking at which the shooters had to aim. The winner was the shooter who got closest to the mark.

In the middle of the 19th century, turkey shooting became popular. The rifles were equipped with heavy barrels and telescopic sights were used that allowed the turkey's head to be targeted. A tree trunk was permitted to stabilize the weapons.

The first years

left:
Aiming requires intense concentration. Kelbly precision Bench Rest weapons are among the best of their type.

With the introduction of the metallic cartridge, this type of competition became more popular, although there were always people with more traditional tastes who continued to use the older but very accurate muzzle-loading rifles. One of the representatives of the new trend was Harvey A. Donaldson, of Fultonville in New York, a marksman who played a large part in the founding of the Eastern Bench Rest Shooters Association in 1947.

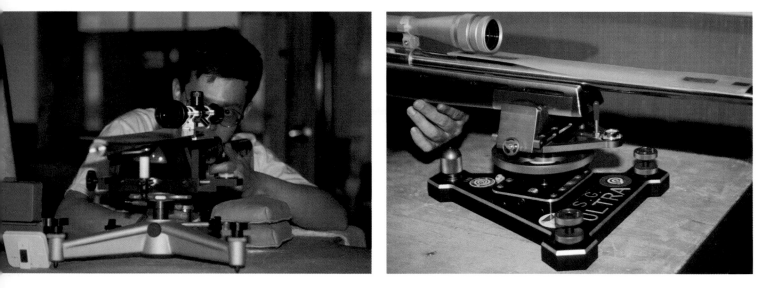

right:
The shooting turret is an essential accessory which stabilizes the weapon and gives more precise groupings.

Shortly afterwards, in 1951, various regional delegations of marksman who loved precision shooting met to found the National Bench Rest Shooter's Association, which brought together all the regional groups in the USA. To this day, the abbreviation NBRSA continues to identify the group that coordinates the diverse sports specialties that are grouped together under the generic denomination of Bench Rest.

They also publish a manual – the United States Bench Rest Rule Book – which was first published in 1998, and a magazine – News,The Voice of Bench Rest – which carries articles of interest to all gun lovers.

The union of man and gun

The main objective of the marksman in Bench Rest is to obtain the closest grouping in series of five or ten shots. In the United States, they shoot at targets located at distances of 100, 200 or 300 yards, whereas in Europe the distances have been adapted to the metric system and are expressed in meters.

In addition, where it is permitted by shooting ranges, competitions are organized over longer ranges, including those where the range is a thousand yards, or a little over nine hundred meters.

The targets have no scoring to determine the results but only certain references that are used to center the viewfinders and to obtain the best possible grouping, independent of the place where the bullets hit.

To determine the real size of the grouping, a micrometer is used to measure the distance that separates the two impacts that are farthest apart. The diameter of the bullet, measured in thousandths of an inch, is subtracted from the measurement to determine the result with absolute precision.

In 100-meter competitions, a standard cardboard target is used, which includes a marking in the lower part to make test shots, known as sighting shots, that do not count and serve only as orientation; in the superior part there is a square mark at which the real shots are aimed. The heavy outlines of the square mark allow the marksman to orientate the reticle of the visor to obtain the best grouping, although details such as wind speed, temperature and environmental humidity must also be considered to calculate the aim with the greatest precision.

left:

In some countries, a variant of Bench Rest is practiced using .22 caliber rifles.

Making the shot

The competitor considers the parameters mentioned above, calculates the most suitable charge and prepares his ammunition. In order to obtain the best grouping it is better to load at the last moment and check to see if any alterations must be made.

right:

Only specifically-designed weapons can obtain the accuracy needed for Bench Rest shooting.

The competitor shoots while seated in a chair or stool and the weapon rests on a solid ambidextrous shooting table that can be used by both right and left-handed people. The table must resist all movements, so that no vibration is transmitted to the weapon, neither in the phase of aiming nor in the firing itself. To obtain maximum stability for the weapon, a turret is placed in the front part of the shooting table.

This consists of a mechanical element that is usually heavy to prevent accidental movement and includes a support for the stock of the rifle and a regulation system to facilitate the aim of the viewfinder on the target. A small leather bag, usually stuffed with sand, is placed at the rearmost part of the stock to obtain a better aim. The elaborate technique also demands that the support areas of the weapon are covered with talcum powder so that they slide without friction during firing and recoil.

I : 32

Competition shooting

The proceedings of shooting competitions are governed by international regulations that are common to all competitions, although in certain countries complementary shooting competitions are organized to introduce young and novice shooters to the discipline.

The most specialized variety is known as Varmint shooting. In this competition, very elaborate long arms, with high quality materials, designs and performance are used, because the objective is to obtain the most closed groupings with a series of shots. This competition is divided into Light Varmint for arms that weigh under 4.767 kilograms and Heavy Varmint for arms that can weigh up to 6.129 kilograms. These weights include the rifle, the viewfinder and its mount and all the extra elements that are added to the weapon. The shooting competition consists of five series of five shots, with a maximum time of seven minutes for each series, a more than sufficient time lapse.

Hunting Rifle

A high degree of concentration is essential to producing close groupings.

Hunting Rifle is a discipline that is somewhat less complicated. The objective is to allow hunters or sportsmen who do not possess weapons of a high enough standard for Varmint to compete and also to discover if this type of sport interests them or not.

In Hunting Rifle competitions, the target includes point markings that are used to calculate the score. Two kinds of arms can be used for this discipline. Stock competitions are for weapons of which more than five hundred have been produced, and Open competitions are open to rifles produced in more limited numbers, including custom made models.

Bench Rest competitions have specific regulations. For example, there is a break of a minimum of half an hour between two series and the total setting-up time is limited to ten minutes. Shooters who use wind sensors are allowed to change their position when the organizers change the targets. There is a minimum time lapse of ninety minutes before the competition starts to enable competitors to place the wind sensors and for cleaning and loading the cartridges. The areas designated for these tasks are strictly separated from the public to avoid any interference that can affect the results of the participants.

The closest groupings

Obtaining very close groupings is not easy because factors such as the weapon, the supports, the mood of the shooter, the ammunition and other elements all play an important role.

Although Bench Rest is dominated by men, some women are also attracted by its challenge.

I : 34

Special material

For this reason, specific accessories are used that help shooters to obtain results like those of Pat McMillan of Phoenix (Arizona), one of the famous McMillan brothers, who obtained groupings of 0.009 of an inch when shooting at a distance of one hundred yards and 2.653 inches at a thousand yards.

This level of groupings demands very specialized material and specially developed ammunition such as the ultra precise 6 mm PPC (Palmisano Pindell Cartridge). It is important to use a shooting turret that is adapted to the needs of the shooter and to choose a back support that is adapted to the regulations and lets the stock slide after each firing.

Loading the cartridges is done onsite and it takes time and experience to know the best type of cartridge for each situation.

Other personal effects used by shooters includes a precision chronometer to time the competitions perfectly, a small hammer to fix the turret to the table, and the cartridges that will be required for each of the series. The cartridges are basic in obtaining good results and are usually loaded just a few minutes before each shot to select the adequate charge and weight of the bullet at each moment. It is very important to have high-precision measuring instruments to weigh the charges.

Bench Rest weapons

As in other shooting disciplines, in Bench Rest each shooter chooses those materials – barrels, actions, stocks, etc. – that adapt best to his tastes, economic resources or needs. For this reason, more companies are springing up which specialize in the manufacture of weapons and accessories for Bench Rest shooting.

George Kelbly who won the gold medal in the 1993 World Championships now makes his own rifles together with his three sons. These arms are among the most coveted by Bench Rest shooters and include one of the most precise actions on the market. Other companies such as McMillan or Speedy Gonzalez also offer products of a very high level. However, many sportsmen prefer models that are custom made to suit their personal tastes and using their preferred components.

Whatever the weapon chosen, high quality telescopic sights are essential. One of the best is the Leupold BR-36 target scope with 36x magnification, target knobs and fine crosshairs. A second hand model could cost around 500 dollars. The weapon must be cared for meticulously. The care of the weapon is also very important: after each series of shots, the bore is cleaned using a cleaning rod such as those produced by Dewey, and the action must also be cleaned.

Bench Rest is a type of shooting where the challenge is essentially personal.

As shooters often achieve such close groupings that it is impossible to tell if one bullet has passed through the same hole as another, a backup target is used to ensure that all the shots are accounted for.

With this type of rifle, excellent groupings can be obtained at hundreds of meters. They are suitable arms to bring down buffalos, bison and animals of similar size.

Lever Action Rifles

Lever action rifles

were introduced during the American Civil War to enable troops to fire various shots before reloading. Hunters soon realized the many possibilities of this type of weapon and adopted it for their own needs. Today these weapons are still popular in hunting circles. Their easy handling, rapid firing capacity, robustness that resists the roughest treatment and compact size are some of the best qualities of lever action rifles. The manual action by which the lever introduces the cartridges in the chamber and expels the empty cartridge case allows a better symbiosis with the shooter and evokes memories of past times. These rifles have sufficient power for hunting in wooded areas or participating in a beat.

The Winchester Model 1873 is one of the most famous classic models.

One hundred and fifty years of history

The first rifles using a lever action were introduced in the last years of the first half of the 19th century.

The classic Winchester

One of the first lever actions was the Volcanic. Walter Hunt, its designer, began to work with the founders of Smith & Wesson, Horace Smith and Daniel Wesson, but the initial idea did not prosper and, by 1857, the Volcanic company was bankrupt.

Around this period, other repeating rifles using a manual action were entering production. These included the Spencer carbine, a long arm that shot .52 caliber cartridges at a rate of up to 20 per minute or the Henry rifle, a .44 model that was greatly appreciated during the American Civil War by the Southern troops who claimed: "you charge it on Monday and it shoots all week".

Oliver Winchester bought the manufacturing rights of the Volcanic design and took over Spencer's factory. He improved both designs by adapting them to use metallic cartridges and incorporating a central fire action.
The result was the Winchester 1873 model, a classic weapon that had great commercial success in America. Its design is so good that some manufacturers still continue to produce it.

Other rifles

The Winchester 1873, initially chambered to fire .40-40 Winchester ammunition, was soon imitated by competitors who adopted a similar mechanical design. One of these competitors was the Marlin Company, which opted for a modified lever action that expelled the empty cartridge cases to the right – the Winchester expelled them upwards – thus allowing scopes to be fixed on the action mechanism, although scopes of those days were long ungainly things which were used only on target rifles and were uncommon.

These and similar options that appeared in other countries became popular among hunters and the military. The Winchester, adapted to the .30-30 caliber, for example, was widely used in the Mexican revolution led by Pancho Villa. Spain produced the Tiger carbines, a variant of the Winchester 1892 model. In Belgium, FN designed lever action models and in America, Savage introduced a model designed to fire its most powerful cartridges.

Over time, replicas of these guns were introduced onto the market, including those made by the Italian company Uberti or the Brazilian company Rossi. These are generally cheap, well made arms that work well.

Advantages and disadvantages

All these weapons have interesting qualities although they also have their limitations due to the characteristics of the firing action. The generally compact design that allows easy carrying and the reduced weight are positive qualities. Its short length helps to aim quickly and allows optimal use of the rear and front sight, although compact viewfinders also allow a quick aim.

The simplicity of use, reliability and low price are some of the reasons why lever action rifles are very attractive for hunters.

I : 40

The quickness and ease of repeat firings and the fact that the conception of the action allows new cartridges to be loaded and fired without having to acquire the target again are also advantages.

The Henry is a lever action rifle with an excellent polygonal barrel that gives it its characteristic accuracy.

Another positive aspect that characterizes these arms is their general simplicity, which keeps the price low. The market offers designs starting at about four hundred euros, although the price of more elaborate models is much higher. This low cost makes them attractive and economic hunting weapons.

Different calibers

The cartridges of the lever action designs are usually stored in a feeding tube parallel to the barrel, although some designs have conventional magazines. In the first type, pointed cartridges have to be used to prevent the accidental detonation of the shotgun primer of the bullet that precedes them.

Due to this and because the action locking elements can seem less solid than those of other designs, cartridges like the .38 Special, .357 Magnum, .30-30, .44-40, .44 Remington Magnum, .375 Winchester or .444 Marlin

One negative aspect is the limitation on the size and caliber of the cartridge, which is defined by action and the storage systems. More recent models have been adapted to shoot very powerful ammunition.

Some people believe that these weapons are less accurate than semiautomatic or bolt action weapons but, as with so many aspects of shooting, this must be put down to individual taste and preference.

have been introduced. The lightness of their tips, that can weigh 250 grains, and their configuration, allows hunters to bring down a large part of European and North American game.

To give this range of rifles a new potential, new cartridges are being introduced with much greater initial velocity and high muzzle energy. These cartridges can be used for bigger prey such as elk or bears.

Among the most recent introductions are the .45-70 whose bullets weigh 300 grains and has a muzzle speed of 550 meters per second, the .450 Marlin which has a bullet weighing 350 grains or the .458 Winchester Magnum, with bullets weighing 500 grains and a velocity of over six hundred meters per second and a kinetic energy that can bring down the largest game, including elephants.

Models equipped with magazines include those adapted for ammunition such as the .30-06 Springfield and the .300 Winchester Magnum, heavy ammunition designed to shoot down big game at medium and long range.

Modern production

Various companies still produce this popular type of rifle. They are very good hunting arms, with simple handling that does not require much training.

The big manufacturers

The American companies produce the majority of the different models of lever action rifles on the market today. The present leader is the Marlin company, with a wide range of models and high levels of sales. They produce about one thousand five hundred rifles a day, although they can produce three thousand pieces at peak moments.

Their catalogue includes models like the 1895M, the 1895G Guide Gun or the recent 1895RL. The 1895M fires the .450 Marlin and has small holes in its muzzle that compensate for muzzle flip.

The 1895G model shoots the .45/70 Government that is very popular in the USA, whereas the 1895RL, which was introduced to the market in the last quarter of 2004, can shoot two of the most powerful cartridges: the .480 Ruger and the .475 Linebaugh.

The company also produces six types of the 336 Model, four types of the 1894 Model and a model that shoots .410 shotgun cartridges.

The other big American manufacturer is Winchester, which has a great tradition and fame in the production of lever action rifles. Its star model is the Winchester 94, which has been produced since the 19th century, although some modifications of the hand guards or the barrel have been introduced.

Other lever action rifles include the Trails End series, the Timber design that is adapted to the .450 Marlin and the classic Legacy that has a 24" barrel and a maximum capacity of twelve cartridges.

Other Winchester models include the 9417/22 model which fires light cartridges, such as the .22 Winchester Magnum or the .17 HMR. They also offer seven rifle models that fire .410 ammunition and incorporate Truglo front sights that allow better aiming in bad light.

The Custom Limited Edition New Generation Model 94 is a special gun from the Winchester Custom Shop, with fine engravings on the receiver and an improved ergonomic stock.

Detail of the muzzles of two lever action rifles and the arrangement of the tubular magazine parallel to the barrel.

Other manufacturers

The best known product of the Belgian company, Browning, which has a large manufacturing plant in the United States, is the BLR Lightweight '81 lever action rifle. This is a more modern rifle with details such as a removable magazine with capacity for three or four .308 or .30-06 cartridges and advanced sights. Its action case is made in aerospace aluminum to make it lighter for easier carrying.

More recent rifles are those produced by Henry Repeating Arms, a small company located in Brooklyn in New York and headed by the Imperato family, which offers interesting and well-finished rifles. They make models like the Big Boy, which has a 20" octagonal barrel and fires .44 Magnum, .44 Special or .45 Colt ammunition, with a tubular magazine which can hold up to ten cartridges. They also offer models which fire the modern .17 HMR and produce the Lincoln, a

The Yellow Boy is an accurate rifle that has been in production for over a century.

variant of the Henry 1860 model which has a rear sight fixed to the action case and a heavy 24"barrel.

The designs of the Italian company Uberti are generally replicas of long arms which enjoyed great success in the past. It offers excellent reproductions of the Henry rifles that lack hand guards and have a heavy, polygonal barrel for long distance shooting.

Finally, the Brazilian company, Rossi, also offers several lever action models that are based on models such as the Winchester 1892, but at a price that is about 30% lower. Although the low price is also reflected in the finish, they have sold really well because they offer a wide range of models and finishes. The present offers are centered on the 65, 67 and 175 models. The 175 has a polygonal barrel and also has a variant made of stainless steel.

Many of the present lever action models were developed in the last decades of the 19th century and had their baptism of fire in the Wild West.

The right hand of the firer moves the lever action while the left one holds the weapon in an almost instinctive movement.

Knight's Manufacturing's
SR-25 is a prized weapon that
is difficult to obtain because
the company only produces a
small number. Its high price
has not dented its popularity.

Tactical Weapons

In recent decades

there has been a remarkable increase in the number of companies that produce elements and accessories which modify rifles into high accuracy weapons, adapting them for tactical police or military missions. Because of this increase in offers, many companies have specialized in transforming rifles. More and more gunmen and hunters are interested in this type of offer which is also used by some of the most famous special units as they are weapons that have the accuracy and firepower needed by many sportsmen and, more importantly, are well adapted to civilian gun laws.

I : 46

Tactical adaptations

At first sight, the difference between a normal hunting rifle and a tactical one is small and could seem insignificant. However, the capabilities that these changes bring is another thing altogether.

Meticulous manufacture

Tactical rifles are normally manufactured in small, specialized gunshops, although more and more large companies have decided to produce this type of long arms, employing craftsmen for the task.

The transformation is usually based on a semiautomatic or bolt action model, depending on the tastes of the client or the transformations that have already been carried out on the model. There are increasing numbers of models that aim to satisfy all types of buyers.

The manual bolt action is the most popular because of its simplicity

and possibilities of transformation. However, semiautomatic models are becoming more popular since they are almost as accurate as manual weapons and can fire many shots consecutively. The Remington 700 is the most popular bolt weapon because its concept and qualities are an ideal starting point for the transformation.

Barrels

The basic process is that of replacing the original barrel with a Mach type barrel which is heavier, resized and rifled to improve accuracy. These factors improve the results but increase the weight of the weapon by more than a kilogram.

The shorter 20" barrels are more popular than the longer 22", 24" or 26" barrels even though these are better for firing at a distance over five hundred meters. Because these barrels are very thick, they

The AR-10T is the model with the greatest accuracy produced in America by the Armalite company.

are often grooved on the exterior to reduce weight and improve cooling. To improve accuracy and regularity in the impact of the bullets, the barrel must reach and maintain a certain temperature.

Other changes

An ergonomic stock that facilitates contact between the long weapon and the shooter can also be introduced. The options include very high-quality models – such as those made by McMillan or H&S Precision – and less elaborate stocks that are cheaper and easier to obtain.

In general, the newest stocks use materials like Kevlar, synthetic graphite or other polymers that are easy to shape and are characterized by their resistance and reduced weight.

This type of materials also allows the choice of different colors and the camouflaging of the weapon. Some options include an aluminum housing which gives greater rigidity and improves the action mechanisms. The stocks are very open in the front part so that the barrel does not touch them and can vibrate freely after firing.

Other details such as front mounts to fix a bipod, rubber butt plates to reduce recoil or mounts for all sorts of accessories are usually incorporated in this type of weapon.

Customizing

The professional gunsmith, who, when adapting weapons by hand, is also known as a customizer, must take special care when installing the different elements. He will have to apply a special treatment to make the mechanisms work smoothly and with precision. He can also introduce personal transformations such as more robust cartridge case extractors or the possibility of feeding the cartridges by magazines.

Fixing the barrel to the action requires special care. The tension applied to the joint is important to maintain the necessary rigidity and accuracy, which can be affected when the barrel and action are not firmly fixed to the stock. To fix these two elements and form a firm block, precision screws or synthetic resins can be used.

Models like these bolt action rifles of the Sniper series are made by the CZ company in the Czech Republic.

DSA produces various options based on the FAL. The tactical versions are noted for their excellent performance at a low price.

I : 48

A bolt action rifle customized for maximum accuracy, with a grooved 24" barrel.

Custom-made guns are now manufactured by craftsmen in many countries.

The Springfield Armory semiautomatic M25 White Feather is known for its performance and the quality of its finish.

Work on the trigger is important to obtain a clean and short trigger movement and to maintain the weight within the desired limits. These elements are important because bad quality triggers could cause a misfire. A specially conceived firing action can be added to the tactical rifle to adapt it to the needs of the user.

A wide range of options

There is a wide and very diverse offer of tactical rifles as more and more companies begin to manufacturer this type of weapon.

Superb manufacture

Various companies offer products renowned for their technical quality.

The internationally renowned British company, Accuracy International, sells its precision arms in various civil, police and military markets. In addition to its AW and AWP ranges of rifles, which are of superior quality and have a very elaborate ergonomic stock, the company now offers the cheaper AE model with a simpler action and barrel.

The company also sells the AICS kit, which consists of a stock that can be adapted to a Remington 700 action and a high precision barrel.

The Belgian company, FN, promotes models which were originally made by the American company, Winchester, or the French firm, PGM Precision, which they manufacture under license.

German models include the Blaser R93 Tactical and Erma Sr-100, which have had limited success. Heckler & Koch has opted for models like the PSG-1 or MSG-90, which are very popular among American gunmen who have been able to acquire them without any problem.

The SSG from the Austrian company, Steyr, the CZ700 and 750 sold by the Czech company, Ceská Zbrojovka, or the Trg-21 and Trg-41 produced by the Finnish company, Sako are also well made guns which sell all over the world.

Low cost models

The American market offers interesting products at a very competitive price. Guns based on the Remington 700 action have sold widely. By adapting the Remington 700, one can obtain weapons that are able to make groupings of ½ MOA (Minute of Angle) or less, which means that three or more shots are made at a target located up to one hundred meters away and that the impacts are grouped in a circle with a diameter of a little over a centimeter.

The products of companies like H-S Precision, McBross or Robar are of better quality, and thus more expensive. Robar, directed by Robert A. Barkman and located in Phoenix, Arizona, maintains an excellent reputation for

its customized high precision arms. The SR90 model allows total ergonomic regulation and groupings near to ¼ MOA. The SR100, based on a new British linear type action, is the most recent offer.

H-S Precision offers several options. The Pro-Series 2000 action is a system that has been designed with the help of a CAD/CAM process to obtain the most satisfactory results. Models like the TTD (Tactical Take-Down) which can be broken down into two parts, the HRT (Heavy Tactical Rifle) which has a long 24"barrel, or the RDR (Rapid Deployment Rifle) which is available with two stock options, are available using this system.

The popularity of tactical weapons has lead to the customizing of models based on simple carbines.

I : 50

Heckler & Koch's MSG-90 is made in Germany. It is semiautomatic, very accurate and has great firepower. For these reasons, civil sales are restricted in some countries.

The catalogue of McBross Rifles, owned by one of the McMillan brothers, offers products like the MCRT Tactical, which includes a patented bolt action and is adapted to shoot the powerful .338 Lapua Magnum.

Its price of three thousand euros is reasonable when compared to the price of four thousand five hundred euros for the TAC-50, which can be optimized to use 12.70x99 mm cartridges.

The recent DS-MP1, made by DSA, is of excellent quality and has an accuracy comparable to higher-priced custo-mized arms.

Semiautomatic rifles

Many of the previously described rifles include a manual action in which the gunman introduces a cartridge into the chamber and facilitates the extraction of the empty cartridge case once shot.

More and more sportsmen are opting for the semiautomatic configuration in which this process is carried out by the rifle without intervention of the gunman, especially because these options have almost the same accuracy and reliability as bolt action rifles. The American company, Armalite, has a good quality AR-10 range that includes two Target models, one with a 24" barrel and another with a 16" barrel. Both are very high quality models with maximum accuracy.

DSA proposes a series of interesting designs based on the action of the Belgian FAL rifle, although with greatly improved performance. The SA58 Gray Wolf model is the top of the range, with floating hand guards, a pistol grip and an ergonomic stock. The simpler SA58 Predator and SA58 Bull Barrel are arms with certain tactical qualities.

The best product in this class of arms is the Knight's Manufacturing's SR-25, which is so good that it is used by the American Special Forces. Like the previous models, it is chambered for the .308 Winchester caliber, and can achieve groupings inferior to ½ MOA. It is available in 16", 20"or 24" barrel versions, its hand guard includes accessory mounts and the trigger is smooth and short to obtain maximum accuracy.

Following the success of the SR-25, other semiautomatic options based on the conception of the AR military rifle and adapted to the .308 have appeared. Springfield Armory has even added the M25 White Feather, a new version of the M21, to its range.

Hunting Rifles

In the world

there are several million fans of small and big game hunting. The size of the animals hunted varies from birds and small game to elks and elephants, but all require the purchase of some type of long arms that offer the characteristics necessary to be able to shoot down the prey. These characteristics vary greatly, depending on parameters such as the physical location of the animals in various types of terrain, the training of the user, how much someone wants to spend, and, of course individual preferences. These factors add up to a wide spectrum of different needs.

The long weapons used in hunting must support the rigors of the wildest hunting locations.

I : 54

A wide range of choices

The number of hunters who select their rifles based on previous knowledge or on the advice given by gunsmiths is increasing as sportsmen demand ever-greater quality from the weapons they buy.

Models for all tastes

The different options in models and actions are conditioned by factors such as the location and the type of prey.

Hunting from a hide is not the same as participating in a beat. Chasing wild boar is very different to hunting an elephant.

Shooting down a roe deer in a hunting reserve has nothing in common with the needs of those who practice Varmint hunting where people shoot small pests such as rats and squirrels at a range of hundreds of meters.

Because of these differences, the sportsman must look for the weapon or weapons that are ideal for his needs. Details such as physical qualities, price and the location where the weapon is going to be used must all be considered.

The type of cartridge to be used should also be selected carefully, making sure that it is neither underpowered nor too powerful.

Other factors to consider are whether it is better to use a manual bolt action or a semiautomatic one, or fixed sights or an optical sight.

Once these factors have been thoroughly studied, the moment has come to choose the weapon.

The present range of rifles includes the following:

- the single shot rifle that has just one chamber and must be fed with a new cartridge each time it is fired;
- the double Express rifle developed to hunt large game,
- bolt action rifles that require the intervention of the hunter to introduce the cartridge in the chamber or to expel the empty cartridge case;
- black powder rifles;
  semiautomatic rifles of various types which expel the cartridge automatically and feed a new one into the chamber;
- lever rifles that have manual feeding using a linear operation mechanism.

These different options are represented by many different models which each have certain advantages. Power, firing speed, capacity of the cartridges, etc., should all be considered, as should the capacity of a specific model to accommodate different types of accessories.

Within this range of options, choosing which is best is a difficult and hazardous task. The novice hunter should weigh up all the information possible, especially by listening to experienced hunters, before making a decision. However, even experts can be wrong.

In the end, personal experience of different conditions and locations will, in time, teach you which gun is right for you.

In any case, hunters should remember that personal tastes often lead to what could be considered irrational decisions. For example, it is not uncommon to find hunters using Express rifles for hunting wild boar when experience tells us this type of rifle is better for hunting larger animals such as elephants.

There are infinite types and models of long arms used for hunting, with more appearing every year.

I : 56

Big game hunting

The types of rifle suitable for this type of hunting are long arms conceived and designed following the basic configuration of side-by-side and over-and-under shotguns, although their barrels have been adapted so that they can shoot the most powerful metal jacketed cartridges, which can bring down any animal. However, these weapons are big and heavy, with weighty barrels and locking actions able to support the high pressures that are generated when firing.

Among the many options available to hunters worldwide, one of the most prestigious is the German company Krieghoff. Their range includes the Classic model, available in a chambered version for options such as the .375 Holland & Holland, or the Classic Big Five model, which was designed after taking into consideration the advice of professional or expert safari hunters and can be used to hunt the biggest animals. It can be adapted to fire the very powerful .500 Nitro Express cartridge.

Another popular type of hunting gun are those made in the small Italian town of Gardone Val Trompia where the Zanardini Armi company has its headquarters and distributes products that are well-known throughout the world. Its Express models include the Bristol and Oxford side-by-side guns and the Könic over-and-under model. It is possible to select engravings on the action, the barrel length and the cartridge type – the best is probably the .416 Rigby.

The Beretta company is also Italian. Its range includes various rifles in the S689 series which are equipped with over-and-under barrels. The models include the Gold Sable and Silver Sable II, which receives an exterior coating of nickel to resist all types of weather.

The Belgian company, Browning, offers several Express arms. These include models like the CCS 25 Express rifle, with the wooden parts made of walnut. The CCS 25

Single shot weapons are popular in some circles. They are accurate and effective, even though they must be reloaded.

Detail of the bolt action of a single shot weapon, one of the many types of hunting gun.

Detail of the locking action of weapon made by the German manufacturer Blaser, showing the engravings that characterize the products of this firm.

has all the characteristics that distinguish Browning guns such as meticulous finishing, great user safety, reliability and strength for life-long service. This highly specialized rifle is primarily intended for the experienced hunter. Browning also manufactures the CCS .375 developed for the big-game .375 H&H caliber and equipped with a shock absorber in its stock, and the CCS Herstal which is based on the action of the B25 shotgun and incorporates an exclusive scope mount system.

The quality of American bolt action rifles is widely appreciated. Remington is known for its options based on the mechanism of the 700 model, which is a real classic in constant evolution. The most recent model is the XCR (Xtreme Conditions Rifle) which includes a TriNyte Corrosion Control System and synthetic stocks to resist the fiercest rain, snow or cold.

In addition, some models are being chambered to accommodate the new 6.8 Remington SPC cartridge which offers a tight trajectory and moderate recoil.

Chapuis guns are also widely used. Their range consists of the Exel, which is a boxlock with large side reinforcement and a barrel length of 600 mm with parallel double hooks, a front scope base and a pistol grip stock with Monte Carlo cheek piece, the Ugex with double set trigger, the luxury Artisan model and the Super Orion Excellence that stands out because of its automatic blitz-type mechanism with automatic unlocking and fine English scroll engraving.

The big game model of the Spanish company Ego of Eibar is a worthy representative of this country. Finally, the British company Holland & Holland produces very high quality arms. One of the most characteristic models is adapted to fire .600 Nitro cartridges. The high quality and hand manufacture is reflected in the price, more than thirty-six thousand euros. The waiting list to buy one of these guns is over a year long.

Different proposals

The market is both traditional and changing: traditional because the basic characteristics remain unchanged in spite of the fact that many decades have passed since their introduction; changing because models appear and disappear from the market with increasing frequency.

Single shot weapons

Single-shot weapons have a chamber for one cartridge only and one barrel. The cartridge is introduced into the chamber by hand. Accuracy is essential as reloading will cost vital seconds. This type of gun is quite popular in central Europe, and there are various European manufacturers.

Hunting guns are often engraved in their actions or mechanisms.

To kill prey such as elk or fallow deer at distances greater than one kilometer, rifles adapted to the .50 Browning caliber are ideal.

Blaser offers the K-95 with twenty-two different options of caliber and Krieghoff specializes in the different engravings of the Hubertus series.

Among the most spread single shot options in the United States are the Ruger N°1, available in six different models and twenty-three different calibers; the Mossberg SSi-One which includes a heavy barrel.

The guns produced by the New England Firearms company include models chambered for light ammunition like the .223 Remington, the .45-70 Government and the .22-250 Remington.

The Shorty, produced by the German company SO Weapons, is a modern option with a "bullpup" configuration, where the locking action is in the back part of the weapon and the trigger under the center of the barrel, thereby reducing the overall length to only 87 cm.

Similar in conception and size is the Italian Stradivari of the Fabbrica Armi Valle Susa. This rifle has three options with barrels of 500, 600 or 740 mm.

The length of the most compact weapon is 57 cm and the longest one measures 81 cm. It includes details such as an elevated metallic base for the sight, a modified stock that acts as a cheekpiece and manual feeding of the cartridge. The Zanardini Armi company also includes several single shot rifles in its catalogue. The Fuchs A has an ergonomic stock and an action that is decorated by hand, the Fuchs B is adapted to support the pressures generated by the most modern cartridges, and the Prinz has three different options.

Black powder

This type of propellant is used both for muzzle-loading weapons and for breech-loading arms. Ruger offers several options for the 77/70 model. Austin & Halleck, a Missouri, USA company, makes the 320 LR which has a stock that is made of synthetic material and a large 26" barrel. Thompson Center Arms specializes in designs like the Fire Hawk that has a central ignition system.

Laws on hunting differ from country to country and greatly influence the choice and development of weapons.

The big manufacturers can choose from a wide range of stocks for their long arms.

Accessories

Both sport and Informal shooting

and hunting require the use of an adequate weapon. The different types of rifles, carbines or shotguns are usually complemented by a series of accessories that help the shooter to obtain closed groupings and a precise aim, whether they are hunting for elephants on the plains of Africa or shooting rats in their own backyard.

Accessories for every need

Every year various international exhibitions are organized which present the best of new and established guns and all their accessories. The most important fairs are probably the American Shot Show, the German IWA and the Italian EXA. These fairs attract several hundred exhibitors – the last edition of the Shot Show attracted around one thousand seven hundred – and act as a magnet for gun lovers and enthusiasts eager to see the latest developments in their sport.

Ear protection is essential when shooting with live fire.

A wide range of products

At these gun fairs, enthusiasts can find the most varied range of weapons and accessories ranging from simple devices aimed at a wide public to specialized components destined for experts or professional shooters.

The products on offer range from basic elements such as straps and carrying cases for rifles and shotguns, to various types of camouflage for shooters, their guns and equipment, optronic and telescopic sights, viewfinders, binoculars and telescopes, high-power lamps, lanterns, torches, laser beams, and cleaning kits for maintaining actions and barrels in perfect conditions.

Other products on sale at the fairs include maps, skinning knives, special shooting gloves, gunsafes, etc.

These products are also sold in gunshops and by catalogue and, increasingly on the internet. In Europe, for example, Frankonia has a well-known catalogue, while in the United States, Brownells or Numrich Arms are well-known names.

Many accessories are manufactured by small companies which often specialize in just one type of product, such as sights or gun cases.

Increasingly, hunters are using illuminated sights for easier aiming in bad light.

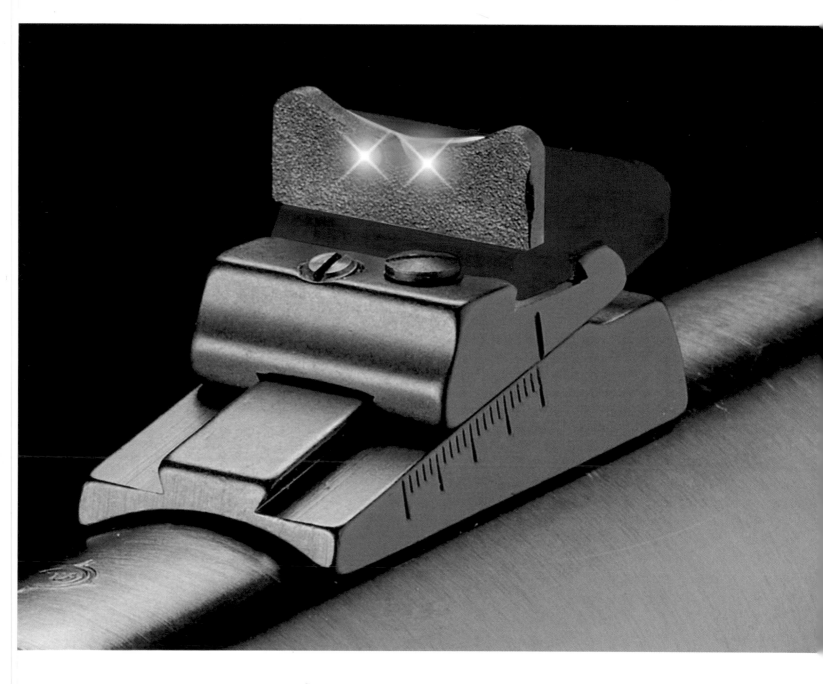

Savage continue to add new models to the Varminter range.

Savage Rifles

The American company

Savage Arms Incorporated, specializes in the production of a wide range of rifles and carbines distributed from their plant located at 100, Springdale Road in Westfield, Massachusetts. They specialize in manufacturing bolt action rifles of impeccable operation and excellent quality. With their general performance and good price, they are aimed at hunting and sport shooting fans, mainly in the United States.

I : 70

The machinery of the different work areas includes old winches and milling machines and designs that are controlled with digital processors.

Careful manufacture

The company directed by Ronald Coburn has a long tradition dating from the introduction of its first model in the 18th century. Since then, they have produced a wide variety of weapons including pistols, shotguns, carbines, rifles and medium-caliber machine guns for military airplanes.

Manufacturing plants

Currently, production is divided between the larger main factory, which was built in the 1960s, and a smaller satellite factory in Lakefield in Canada.

The factory includes various production areas which employ over three hundred people, many of whom have been with the company for many years and are highly specialized in tasks that vary from choosing the raw materials, – mainly steel and wood – to the final post-production tests undergone by each weapon.

The company mainly supplies the civil market, especially hunters. In addition to the North American market, the company has distribution points in Germany, Australia, the United Kingdom and many other countries.

Work areas

The production of center fire rifles takes place in the Centerfire area of the factory. Current production is somewhat down on previous decades, although around three hundred rifles a day are still produced, which adds up to an annual total of about one hundred thousand units.

The manufacturing process is progressive and begins with the reception of the steel tubes of diverse thicknesses. First, the tubes are cut to the right length for 20" or 26" bolt barrels, and for the bolt actions, which are manufactured with specialized machinery such as winches and milling machines. Older machines are used in conjunction with modern computer controlled machine tools.

The manufacture of the barrel starts with the piercing of a central hole, fluting it based on the diameter of the bullets which the rifle will use. After this, the outer turning gives it its required profile and a thermal treatment based on the combination of heat and chemical agents is applied to give the barrel its characteristic bluish patina. Stainless steel barrels, which are becoming increasingly popular do not require chemical treatment, although they are polished or blasted with fine sand in order to give them a shiny or mat finish.

The action

The different action models which characterize their wide range are produced in another area. Basically, without going into the details of the differences between cartridges of a different caliber, they are based on a short or long action, with the long action being more appropriate for bigger and more powerful ammunition. The manufacturing process has not changed much in the last few years except for some details due to the conception of new models. A muzzle with internal reduction that protects the rifling from an accidental blow, redesigned safety

New models, such as those for left-handers are constantly being introduced.

levers, the possibility of incorporating a muzzle brake to reduce recoil and muzzle flip, a stock that is fixed to the action by dual pillar bedding or an AccuTrigger-type trigger are a few examples of recent developments.

Those modifications are applied when the bolt action is joined to the barrel. After this, the front sights or the mounts for optronic telescopic sights are added.

Manufacturing is divided into different production areas for efficiency and quality control.

After this, the metallic elements of the gun, are transferred to another work area, where they are fixed to the stock, which may be made of normal or laminated wood or synthetic materials, depending on the qualities and characteristics of each model.

Next, details like the rubber butt plate or the removable magazines are added. The penultimate step consists of laser engraving of the model and series number and ensuring that the rifle is up to standard.

A structured process

Special accessories or finishes desired by some clients are added after the marking of the serial number; these extra individual elements increase the price of the finished product.

For this reason, the company offers "package series", which are modified models including, for example, viewfinders so that the user can shoot or hunt without limitations and without other modifications.

The last phase of the manufacturing process is the acid test that verifies that the weapon respects the strict security and accuracy parameters that Savage demands.

A cartridge with a pressure charge one and a half times the normal charge is shot to validate the resistance of the weapon. Finally, the rifle, a set of protective earplugs, a security that blocks the trigger, a manual and the targets for the initial test are packed in a cardboard box for transport from the factory to retail outlets.

The whole process can be carried out in one day because the different work areas are structured so that each part moves sequentially from one area to another until the finished rifle is produced. This enables Savage to maximize output while retaining control of quality at all times.

A wide range

The 2004 Savage Catalogue contains a range of rifles and carbines. In addition there is a range of Custom Shop offers for clients with special needs.

Accuracy and reliability

Savage rifles are widely used by hunters and other gun lovers due to their accuracy and quality. The two most recent models are the Varminter Low Profile, the latest additions to the model 12 bolt action range.

The Varminter Low Profile comes equipped with Accu Trigger and a short action. It is available in .223 Remington, 22-2250 Remington and .204 Ruger calibers. The overall length is just over 46 inches and the barrel length is 26 inches and the weight is around 10 lbs. The stock is dual pillar bedded and has a low profile. The gun features a stainless barreled action and a free-floating, button-rifled barrel. There are also single-shot versions and a new variant adapted for use by left handed shooters.

The BVSS models are similar. There are four different versions with short or long actions adapted for left- or right-handed people and the stock includes an ambidextrous Wundhammer palm swell.

The Model 12FVSS also has a short action and is available in .223 Remington, 22-250 Remington, .308 Winchester, .270 WSM and .300 WSM calibers. It has a black synthetic stock with checkering, a twenty-six inch barrel, and comes at a price of around six hundred and seventy dollars.

The 16/116 range includes the Model 116FCSAK of the Weather Warrior series, which has a 22" or 24" barrel including the adjustable muzzle break. The long action can be adapted to various calibers including the .338 Win Mag.

Savage also produce the 11/111 Hunter series with various models for right and left handers. The 10GY Youth model is aimed at young shooters and comes at an economical price of nearly five hundred dollars.

Other models

Savage also produces various models of .22 LR caliber carbines, and semiautomatic rifles such as the Model 64 which are available with synthetic or wooden stocks and in a black satin finish.

The best-known bolt model is the Mark II, a range that includes both simple and expensive options with a laminated wooden stock and heavy barrel. They also offer some models adapted to the .22 Magnum.

The careful treatment applied to the action adds to its quality and attractiveness.

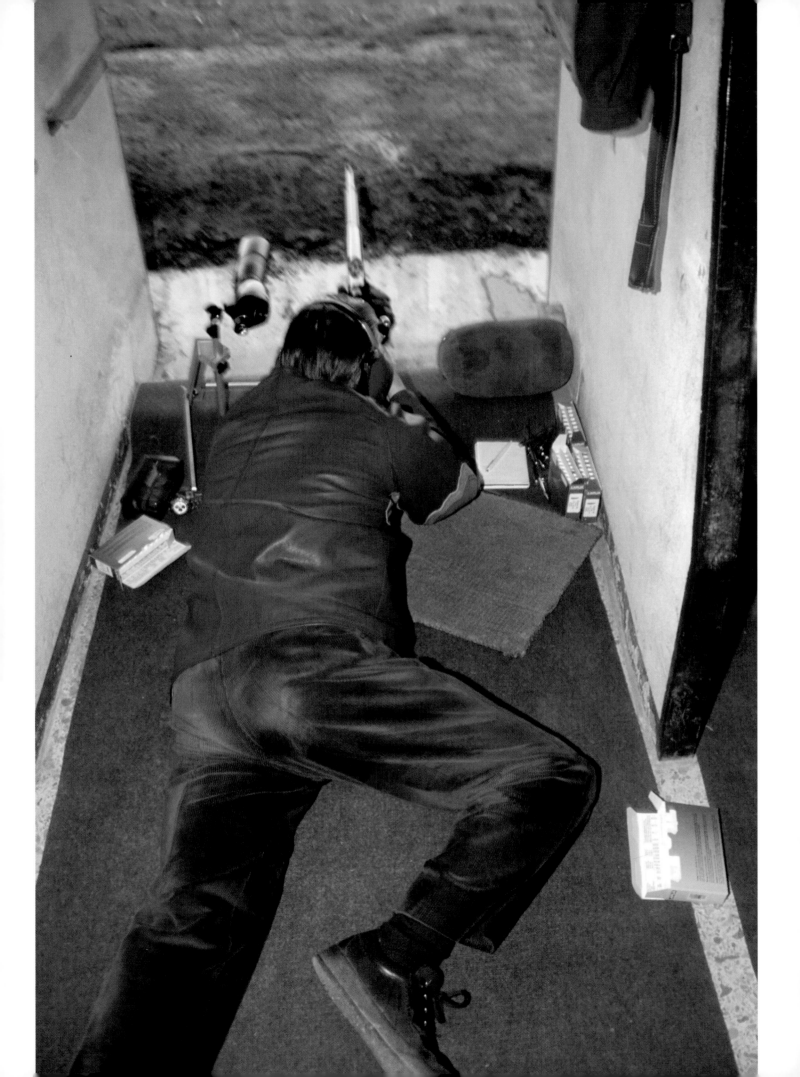

Military rifles for sport shooting

The availability of different models

of rifles that were used by armies of various countries has caused more and more enthusiasts, collectors and sportsmen to choose this type of weapon. They are used in informal shooting sessions or in different types of competitions that admit this kind of weapon. Their design evokes past times and represents a good part of the history of long arms. They can be bought in very good condition and weapons that have often never been used are offered for sale when distributors gain access to some of the reserve stocks held by governments.

In one hundred meter competitions, the shooter assumes a prone position for better aiming.

I : 76

In general, these military rifles are characterized by a careful manufacturing process using high-quality combat-validated materials. They are usually offered at a competitive price, and some models, due to their scarcity, have become collector's items, rising considerably in price. However, gun lovers should know that sometimes it can be difficult to obtain spare parts and ammunition for some of these weapons.

Shooting gloves can help to give the best support to the weapon when aiming.

Bolt action rifles

The majority of military rifles used by shooting enthusiasts use a manual bolt action, a system which has demonstrated its great robustness, remarkable reliability and accuracy.

Military origin

This type of long arms was conceived to equip the infantry, and their design and manufacture followed strict norms. The best materials, basically steel and wood, were used, and the design was ergonomic, in order to provide greater accuracy against long-distance targets. For this reason, they have proved to be very good weapons for participating in competitions where the targets are located at one hundred meters. These qualities, together with the types of ammunition for which they were adapted, have meant that most military rifles are similar, with a wooden stock that covers a good part of the barrel to protect the users from burning their hands when it reaches a high temperature after various shots, a metallic butt plate in the posterior part designed for to protect the rifle from the blows that could be received in battle, a magazine located under the action to facilitate reloading, a front hoop and back fixation to fix a sling that allows a more stable aim and sights, usually including an adapted rear and front sight to allow optimal use of the cartridge shot by the rifle at distances of more than a thousand meters. There is a worldwide market for these pieces, especially in Europe and the United States where these guns are more appreciated due to their historic value and the qualities that allow them to be used in different shooting disciplines and in hunting.

They are also of interest to collectors, who buy weapons with an interesting history that sets them apart from the more characterless modern weapons.

Even so, the numbers of people using this type of weapon is limited, although increasing. One reason may be that there is no Olympic competition for this type of long weapon, although there are certain adaptations.

In Spain, for example, there is an occasional national championship for shooting with military rifles. The contestants go through a series of tests that include six series of ten shots, in a standing position and without support, against silhouette targets at a distance of one hundred meters.

The main difficulties are holding the heavy rifle, the correct alignment of the sights, especially when these begin to vibrate due to the heat of the barrel and the use of ammunition that is most suited to the characteristics of the rifling – the number of striations per inch – that characterizes each mo-

del. If the terrain allows it, shooting contests at a distance of three hundred meters are often organized in which military rifles can be used. In the United States, where there is an enormous amount of space and opportunity for informal shooting in many states, a lot of competitions for long arms, espe-

cially the ones that were used by the American army, are organized.

The shooting distances vary from one hundred to one thousand yards and two similar, semiautomatic models are mainly used: the M1 Garand and its variant with a magazine, the M14.

The military bolt action rifle

However, the most-commonly used weapons have a bolt action, as typified by the mythical M1898 rifle developed by the German company, Waffenfabrik Mauser AG, for the German Army, which is designated as the Gewehr 98.

Originally, it shot 7.92x57 mm ammunition designated the 8x75 Mauser, had a capacity of five cartridges and was 1.255 m long and weighed 4.14 kg. A shorter variant, the M1898 Kurz was also developed. The most-popular model was probably the Kararbiner 98K, an improved version with a modified bolt lever.

The Kararbiner 98K was made by Mauser and other German arsenals such as Amberg, Berlin, Danzig, Erfurt or Spandau to equip the Wehrmacht. The development of this concept, which resulted in a shorter version which was 1.10 m long and weighed 3.86 kg was considered especially suitable for combat, with its optimal weight distribution, and proved its qualities during World War II.

Increasing numbers of shooting enthusiasts are taking up new forms of shooting to accompany more traditional competitions.

The model was even used by the Israelis during their first clashes with the Arab countries.

Various other weapons have been developed based on the original German design, including the Czech 24 VZ, the Israeli transformations for the 7.62x51, the Brazilian model developed by the Berliner Deutsche Waffen und Munitions-Fabriken (D.W.M.) or the Norwegian adaptation that uses the 30-06 Springfield cartridge.

Other models are the Argentinean adaptation for the 7.65x53 mm cartridge, the Mauser M98-38 used by the Iranian army and the Yugoslav carbine M48 with an 8x57 IS caliber, which can easily be acquired in mint condition for around 180 euros upwards, although the price of new German units with factory markings can be much higher.

Logical evolution

Mauser's design, dating from 1892, has served as a reference for many companies that have produced similar models for the European and American markets.

Military rifles are very accurate, even though many of them were designed more than a century ago.

Military bolt actions

The Springfield 1903 model was developed based on the experience of the Cuban War between Spain and the USA. Using captured Spanish Mauser model 1893 rifles as a base, and applying the improvements introduced in the Mauser 1898, such as a third posterior security lug and a bolt safety, a long weapon was designed which was chambered for the 7.62x63 mm and .30-06 Springfield calibers.

Among its many qualities, which led to it being used in the two World Wars, the most important was its accuracy, which derives from the use of a combina-tion of a cartridge with a very tight trajectory, a precision-made 61cm barrel and an exceptional rear sight with settings of 100 to 530 yards. Furthermore, it has excellent mechanical details such as the vertical aim slide with settings of up to 2,850 yards, the five-shot double-feed magazine, the striker pin with two sections, or the action that allows the weapon to be used as a single-shot weapon or as a manual repeating rifle.

The Swedes also based the excellent Carl Gustav 1896 on the German Mauser. The Carl Gustav is much appreciated for its careful manufacture and the advantages

One-hundred-year-old military rifles can be just as accurate in the right hands as more expensive and theoretically superior modern models.

Military rifles are popular in various countries such as the United States, where there are shooting competitions at 600 or 1,000 yards.

derived from the use of 6.5x55 mm cartridges, which are powerful and maintain a very tight trajectory, and for its very useful tangential rear sight which is adjustable for height. Also popular is the Mosin-Nagant 1891/30 model, a weapon designed at the end of the 19th century to equip the Czarist army of Imperial Russia. Its revolving bolt action was developed by Colonel Sergei Mosin, who also added a fixed, single-feed magazine invented by the Belgian brothers Emile and Leon Nagant.

The final design was chambered for the 7.62x54R cartridge, known for its great accuracy and this, together with the 729 mm with four riflings with a turn every 241 mm, make this an accurate and extremely hard-wearing rifle that was able to survive the famous Russian military campaigns that took place on battlefields that were often frozen solid for months. Other, perhaps less well-known military rifle that are available on the civil market but which are mainly bought by specialized collectors include the Finnish Mosin-Nagant M39 with a two-piece stock for stability, and the Nagant Carbine, a shortened version measuring one meter and weighing about 4.1 kg.

Reduced cost

Gun-dealers catalogues often contain more than a dozen different types of military rifles of good quality and performance and which are usually offered at a price that is substantially cheaper than a hunting rifle of equivalent performance. The supply of these models continues to increase and includes rifles like the famed British Enfield, which has many admirers, the French MAS 36 or the Italian Mannlicher-Carcano, which is infamous for having been used to assassinate President Kennedy in Dallas. In spite of their many benefits, the users of this type of rifles must consider that their correct use demands holding the butt plate firmly against the shoulder and that the use of a shoulder sling is advisable because of the strong recoil generated by firing the weapon.

Their actions, which in many cases are worn-in by repeated military use, are robust and resist rough treatment. Various companies specialize in producing replacement pieces which will prolong the life of these historic weapons well into the future.

Detail of a shooting boot. The flat sole ensures a correct position.

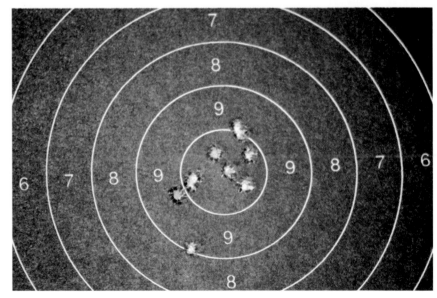

Older military rifles, in the hands of expert marksmen, can yield very close groupings.

Gun makers offer many types and models of carbines, including this model that can broken down for easier carrying.

Carbines

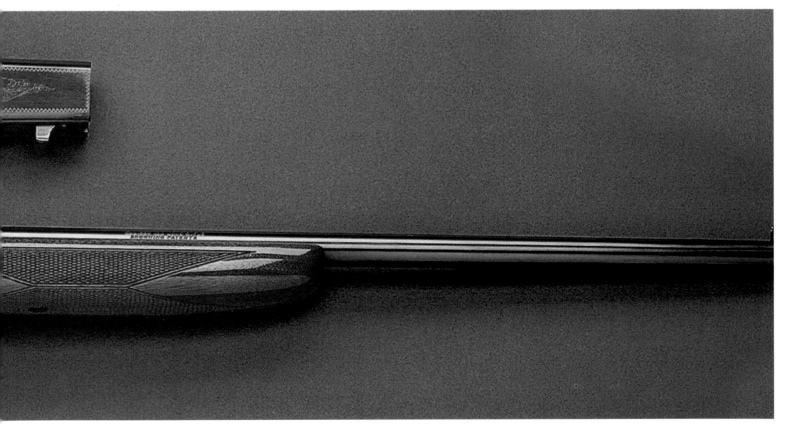

Every year

hundreds of thousand of firearms are sold bearing the name of "carbine". In general, they are weapons which use low power cartridges, especially the .22 Long Rifle. Carbines are used in both Olympic disciplines and informal shooting. Many gun lovers buy them to use as a training weapon or for fun, due to their dynamic qualities and the intrinsic accuracy of many models.

I : 84

Carbines are exceptionally accurate at 50 meters, although they can be used for longer range shooting.

Laws passed by different countries restricting the use of firearms, mean that in some countries these weapons are used for pastimes such as shooting at metal targets or bottles, which is known in the United States as plinking, or small metallic silhouettes. In other countries, such as France, noise suppressors can be bought legally, thus allowing carbines to be used in the countryside or confined spaces without disturbing the peace of those who live nearby. In general, carbines are used for fun. However, many carbines are also used for speciality shooting, including Bench Rest and Olympic disciplines. Carbines are also used in Varmint shooting, a type of shooting popular in the USA among users of these low-cost, low-power firearms. "Varmint" is an etymological corruption of "vermin", and these weapons were originally used to shoot all kinds of pests such as rats and squirrels, although today Varmint rifles are also used in competitions, including Bench Rest.

A wide range of models

The present range of this type of arms is very wide, with prices that can vary from less than three hundred euros for the Russian bolt action models of the TOZ series or the Chinese Norinco, to two thousand euros for a model designed for high-level competition shooting.

The price normally defines the quality of the weapon, but even the cheapest weapons can be very accurate if fired by an experienced and skilled shooter. The intrinsic accuracy of the .22 LR caliber cartridge, which is usually used in carbines, although some use handgun cartridges, enables carbine users to center their shots extremely well, especially when the weapon rests on a support or a telescopic sight is used.

Carbines also allow longer shooting sessions at a reasonable cost. For example, boxes of fifty cartridges can be bought for about three euros, while a box of match-type cartridges cost less than ten euros.

Ample choices

The weapons produced by the Italian company, Adler, became available on the European market during the 1980s. They are carefully manufactured replicas of some of the best-known military assault rifles, such as the American M16, the Soviet Ak-47, the French Famas or the Israeli Galil. Using a semiautomatic action and firing .22LR caliber cartridges, these weapons sold well.

The same concept was adopted by the Fratelli Pietta company, who manufactured a replica of the PPSh submachine gun, which was widely used in the Russian campaign during World War II. It had a circular magazine with a capacity of fifty cartridges and was about 2.5 kilograms lighter than the original model.

Replicas of military carbines, once quite popular, are now no longer produced, having been replaced by other types of guns. One of these options, which is very fashionable in the United States, allows any AR-15 type rifle to be converted into a .22 caliber carbine by replacing the upper receiver with one which includes a thicker, more accurate barrel. The price is a little over three hundred dollars.

The low price and the fact that this weapon shoots cheap cartridges explain the popularity of this semiautomatic option.

New models

Also successful, perhaps unexpectedly, are semiautomatic weapons based on well-known assault rifles from which the possibility of firing in bursts has been eliminated and other small changes, such as the substitution of the folding stock by a fixed stock, introduced.

The Israeli Uzi sub-machine gun or German MP5, for example, are available in an adapted version for civilians. In some cases, longer barrels are used to improve accuracy and in other models magazines with a limited capacity are introduced, as sportsmen do not need as many cartridges as the military or police.

The Uzi and MP5, along with other models, are chambered to use pistol ammunition, especially the 9x19 mm Parabellum and the .45 ACP, which is relatively cheap and is available all over the world. In turn, these features have led to the appearance of kits that enable a handgun to be transformed into a carbine. This involves combining the frame of the handgun with a longer barrel and stock to provide greater range and better accuracy. These kits cost a little over two hundred euros in the countries where they are manufactured, making them a cheap and easy option.

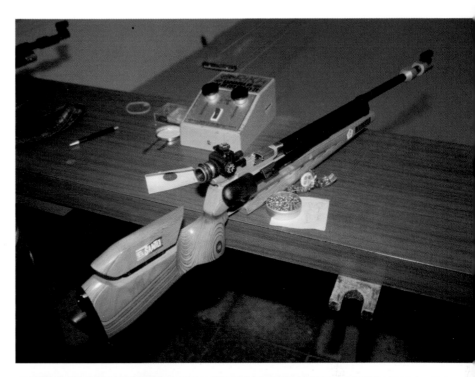

Ten-meter compressed air shooting competitions use models like this. Compressed air carbines are capable of great accuracy.

This .22 LR caliber carbine is used for Action Shooting and incorporates a scope, a high cheekpiece and a muzzle compensator.

Other adaptations

Another type of conversion is represented by the kits that allow some rifles to be transformed to use .22 cartridges, converting them into carbines for informal shooting.

a kit that allows shooting in bursts (when national laws permit it) with models such as the ubiquitous Thompson, famous for its use in war and by gangsters in the USA, probably most notably during the

made in a few minutes at minimal cost and that the converted weapon does not lose its original qualities. If the diameter of the barrel is not adaptable, a subcaliber that is introduced by the bore is used.

Entertainment or sport

The most sophisticated carbines can be used at the highest level of competition due to their remarkable accuracy.

These kits are manufactured by various companies, including the American company, Arthur Cienner, which has the widest range of models and the best performance. Their present range includes

famous "St.Valentines Day Massacre", which is extremely popular among some groups of gun lovers in the United States. The main advantage of this type of kits is that the changes can be

Carbines are ideal for fun shooting and sport shooting, and the many different models are sold all over the world, with some selling in the millions and providing their manufacturers with great success.

This success is also due to the fact that, in some countries, carbines can be bought without many legal or bureaucratic obstacles which may deter some gun lovers. This is because due to their low fire power they are considered as a less dangerous type of weapon.

Different actions

Carbines can use manual actions, (bolt action, lever action, slide action), semiautomatic actions or single shot actions. Manual and semi-automatic action carbines usually have a ten or fifteen cartridge magazine. Some models incorporate a tube parallel to the barrel to store the cartridges and feed the chamber manually or semiautomatically.

All these types of actions have their supporters and detractors. Manual actions are better for sport shooting because of their greater accuracy, especially in competitions between expert marksmen. Semiautomatic carbines have a wider range of uses, as they can be employed both in Action Shooting competitions and in informal sessions shooting at targets at a range of up to 50 meters in any kind of shooting range.

Semiautomatic models

The most-famous semiautomatic carbine is the Ruger 10/22, not only because it has been manufactured since 1964, but also because over four million have been sold to date, making it the best-selling weapon of its kind.

Among its main qualities are the weight of a little over two kilograms, its rapid firing and great reliability, which is due to its special rotating magazine that avoids jamming, and its accuracy, especially in variants equipped with a Target-type barrel.

The present range includes options with 18½ or 20" barrels and synthetic or wooden stocks. There are ten models that shoot the .22 LR and two which shoot the .22 Magnum or the new .17 HMR.

The Remington 597 semiautomatic model is a combination of the most modern technologies. The locking system is reinforced to make it more robust, consistent and precise.

Much of the inner mechanism is treated with a Teflon covering to make firing smoother.

Marlin also includes well-made semiautomatic carbines among its range of long arms.

The various models available are based on the six different variants of the 60 model and on the 795/7000 series.

A fourth interesting option is the Browning SA 22 model, which is a functional weapon that can be broken down easily and is loaded in an unusual way, with the cartridges being stored in the stock.

Sport shooters aiming for the highest degree of accuracy use weapons like these Anschütz carbines whose performance is optimal.

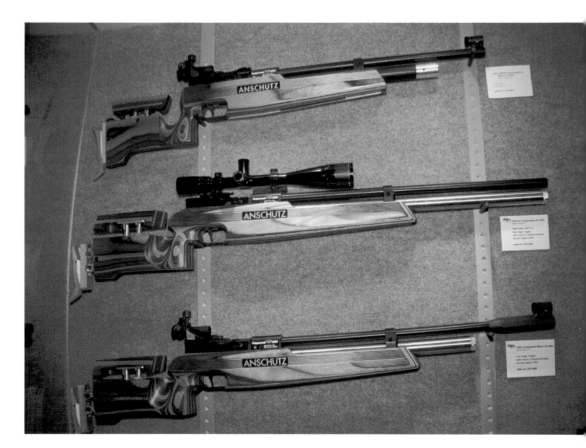

I : 88

Manual and compressed air models

Detail of the manual locking action and the small curved magazine of a carbine, which holds ten .22 cartridges.

The manual Marlin and Savage models are well known to gun lovers. In 2004, Marlin introduced the T-900 firing system that improves the dynamic qualities of the set trigger. It is available in the bolt action 917, 925, 982, 981 or 983 models, a combination of about fifteen different variants that has something for everyone.

The Savage company catalogue is based on four basic models. The Model 93 is available in the traditional .22 LR or the more powerful .22 WMR. The Mark I single shot carbine is a good introductory gun for novices. The Mark II has a magazine with a very pronounced curved shape, while the Model 99 is adapted for longer range shooting.

Among compressed air carbines, Feinwerkbau is, perhaps, the leading company. The weapons comprising the 700 model range are excellently made and range in price from one thousand one hundred euros to around one thousand seven hundred euros.

Walther also make excellent compressed air carbines, including variants of the 300 XT type that have different levels of finish and accessories. The 300 XT shoots 4.5 mm ammunition, the norm for compressed air weapons.

Anschütz manufactures very well-made carbines such as the 9003 Premium type and the 2002 series, which have adjustable triggers, a cheekpiece, a movable butt plate, and modeling to provide support for the left hand.

Among the many other makes of compressed air carbines are the Czech CZ 200 T model and the Austrian Steyr LG 100.

Some pistols, like this Israeli Bull, can be converted into light carbines using kits. The Bull fires 9x19 mm Parabellum ammunition.

Detail of a semiautomatic Erma M1 carbine, a type of weapon which is ideal for informal shooting.

Everywhere in the world competitions are organized in which sport carbines have the role that they deserve.

Sport shooting

Carbines

are used by many gun lovers because they are very accurate and their cartridges are cheap. The great amount of models and variants that are offered by the numerous manufacturers and the wide range of prices, with something to suit all users, adds to their popularity. Because of these qualities, carbines are often used by novice sport shooters. After a while, most sport shooters evolve towards one of the many sport modalities in which a carbine is used. In general, carbines are easy to handle, comfortable to aim and have an excellent accuracy at distances of about fifty meters. For this reason, they are used both in Olympic disciplines and in other types of shooting, ranging from informal "plinking" to target shooting using silhouettes of various animals, which is practiced in many shooting ranges, above all in the United States.

I : 92

Olympic disciplines

Sport shooters normally practice one of the shooting specialties that are governed by the regulations of the ISSF (International Shooting Sports Federation). The various specialties are differentiated by the number of shots that are fired and the type of weapon used.

For example, the target used in shooting competitions with the .22 caliber carbine has a 10 zone that measures a little over a centimeter, with concentric circles around it that indicate scores from 9 to 1, with the lowest score being situated in the circle farthest from the center.

Hitting the bulls-eye demands great concentration.

Fifty-meter range

One of the shooting specialties in which carbines are used is the 3x40 shooting competition for men, in both junior and senior categories.

The weapons can weigh a maximum of 8 kilograms and fire .22 caliber (5.6 mm) bullets. The shooter fires 40 times in a maximum of 45 minutes from a prone

position. The shooter then has ten minutes to adjust the sights, and then fires 40 more shots in 60 minutes in a kneeling position. Finally, the shooter fires 40 times in 75 minutes in a standing position.

The one hundred and twenty competition shots, as well as the test shots used for sighting, are made on the same number of targets to facilitate the count of the impacts and the total score. The present world record is held by the Slovakian shooter Raymond Debevec who obtained 1,186 out of a maximum of 1200 points in 1992. The team record is held by the Austrian team who obtained a total of 3,508 points, the sum of the individual scores obtained by the three team members, in July 2003.

Female competitions

The 3x20 modality is a variation of the 3x40 and is reserved for women, also in junior and senior categories. The arms have a maximum weight of 6.5 kg and the participants fire twenty shots in each of the three positions, prone, kneeling and standing. The maximum time is 135 minutes and the competitors do not have additional time to adjust the carbine between positions.

The world record holder is the Bulgarian Vessela Letcheva, who obtained a total of 592 points in a competition in Munich in June 1995. The Chinese team holds the world record for teams, obtaining a total of 1,754 points during the World Championship in 1998 in Barcelona.

The 50 meter rifle prone discipline is a specialty in which men, woman, female and male juniors can participate, although only men and female juniors are Olympic categories.

The shooter fires from a prone position at a target located at 50 meters. In 75 minutes, sixty competition shots and all the sighting shots must be fired. The weight of the .22 carbines is different for men and women.

Several men have obtained six hundred points, which is the maximum score. In 2003, the Austrian team obtained a total of 1,793 points.

Compressed air carbines

The compressed air carbine is a special model of carbine that uses air to propel small .177 caliber or 4.5 mm bullets. The bullet is loaded manually and the weapon is charged manually by pumping or by transfer from a small magazine in the form of a bottle, which is incorporated in the weapon.

In this type of competition, the target is located at 10 m from the shooter and is formed of a small card with several circles. The target is usually contained in an automatic device, of which there are various types, that enable the targets to be changed rapidly, thereby enabling shooters to fire rapidly in order to comply with the strict time limits imposed in this discipline.

The discipline with the highest number of competitors is the Compressed Air Carbine 60, a specialty restricted to men of any age. The shooter has to fire sixty shots at sixty targets in under one hundred and five minutes. As in similar specialties, the total time includes the preparation of the weapon, the test firings for sighting, etc.

Tevarit Majchacheeap from Thailand obtained a new world record of 600 points in this shooting specialty in 2000. The Chinese team obtained a total of 1,782 points in a shooting competition in October of 2002.

The Compressed Air Carbine 40 competition is open to women. The number of short is reduced to 40 and the time to 75 minutes.

The maximum weight of the arms is 5.5 kg and the trigger does not have a weight limit. The shooter has four test targets for sighting before the real competition begins.

The world record holder is the Korean Sun Hwa Seo, who obtained 400 points in a competition in Sydney in 2002. The Chinese Du, Gao and Zhao are the team world record holders with 1,194 points.

Other disciplines

In addition to the Olympic competitions, there are other types of shooting competitions that are authorized by different federations but have fewer participants.

These carbine competitions include, among others, the Action Shooting competitions organized in the United States, where participants must fire at small metallic objects using carbines that shoot .22 ammunition, generally high speed LR cartridges.

Only elite shooters can compete in national and international championships.

Running target

Running target shooting is one of the disciplines recognized by the International Sport Shooting Federation. In the men's running target event, competitors shoot at a moving paper target from a distance of 10 meters. The event involves a "slow run" and a "fast run". The shooters stand unsupported and shoots in a standing position, starting with his rifle at hip level and raising it only after the target appears. There are also competitions at 50 meters. The 10-meter competitions use compressed air carbines and the 50-meter competitions use .22 caliber carbines.

The weapon, including the telescopic sight, cannot weigh more than five kg. The arms may have an adjustable butt plate and adjustable cheekpiece.

The .22 weapons are closely regulated by the international organization. The inferior part of the butt plate must not have protuberances that surpass 20 mm, the distance between the posterior part of the viewfinder and the muzzle must be less than a meter, the pressure of the trigger must be more than 500 grams and the compensator located in the front part of the barrel must have a diameter inferior to 6 cm.

In 50-meter competitions, which usually take place in enclosed or partially enclosed shooting ranges, the target is the silhouette of a wild boar. The exact point where the shooter has to concentrate his shots is marked on the back of the target. The shooter has to wait until the animal appears in a horizontal trajectory and then aim at the markings. Sometimes the wild boar will go from left to right and sometimes in the other direction. Before the target appears, which is normally observed on a television screen that is linked to a monitor, the shooter has to adopt a waiting position with the weapon directed upwards in the hands. The shooter usually has a marking on his shooting jacket to indicate where he has to position the butt plate.

On sighting the target, the shooter must aim and shoot in less than five seconds, when the target moves slowly and in less than 2.5 when the target moves faster. Men carry out two series of thirty shots at both speeds, whereas women execute two series of 20 shots.

Bench Rest 50

The .22 caliber carbines can be used in the high-precision specialties that are not an Olympic discipline but are included in their corresponding sports federation. This type of arms is centered on BR50 shooting competitions where the carbines are supported on solid shooting tables with the small targets located at fifty meters.

Both bolt action and semiautomatic models are used. The two types use very accurate .22 ammunition, because groupings of the order of 0.25 MOA (Minute Of Angle) or less are necessary to have a chance of winning. The use of powerful telescopic sights to focus on the precise target and to obtain the best possible results is characteristic of this specialty. Furthermore, the set trigger is smoothed so that its activation requires very little pressure.

However, the relatively small mass of the .22 bullets makes them especially vulnerable to the gusts of wind. for this reason, some shooters use different instruments to measure the wind direction and speed in order to make the necessary corrections.

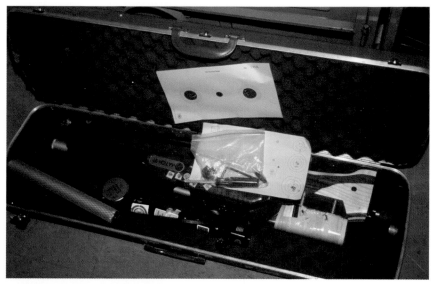

These weapons are normally carried in rugged gun cases that prevent any accidental damage to the gun.

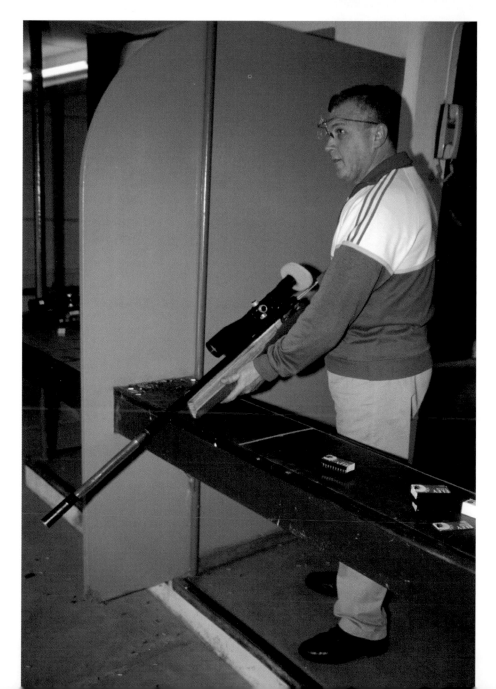

In some disciplines, such as Running Target shooting, with 50 meter targets, the shooter waits for the target to appear before aiming and firing.

Semiautomatic shotguns

Visitors

to some of the international firearms exhibitions, which draw distributors, salesmen and retailers from all over the world, have probably seen the promotional video used by the Italian company, Benelli, to demonstrate the qualities of its products. This video shows a famous American marksmen using a Benelli semiautomatic shotgun. Holding the weapon in his right hand, with his left hand he throws six small ceramic discs similar to those used in clay pigeon shooting into the air, and fires six rapid shots that destroy the discs before the reach the ground. The video serves as an example to both beginners and experienced shooters of the speed and fire power of a semiautomatic weapon, in this case an Italian shotgun with reduced recoil. The mechanisms of this shotgun, as in similar weapons, absorb part of the energy that is released when firing and use this energy for two actions: for expelling the empty shell case and for loading a new shell in the chamber. The shooter only has to move the set trigger to shoot in semiautomatic mode. However, the recoil and muzzle flip associated with semiautomatic firing make sighting and aiming more difficult.

The semiautomatic shotgun can shoot various types of shells and can be used to hunt a wide range of animals.

I : 100

Camouflage is used in this range not only to give greater invisibility but also to provide the weapon with a special look.

Speed and smoothness

The mechanism of semiautomatic shotguns, which some people erroneously continue to call automatic weapons, is based on the incorporation of a series of mechanical elements that eliminate the intervention of the shooter in the reloading process. The shooter still has to introduce the first shell in the chamber, manually or with the help of a device.

Simple design

The first models of this type of long arms were conceived at the end of the 19th century, when the American inventor, John Moses Browning, designed and made a first prototype. His idea was based on a model that was first manufactured in 1903 and of which six million units were made. It incorporated an action that took advantage of the recoil movement of the barrel to expel the empty shell case and to reload another shell.

This type of operation and others that use part of the energy generated by the ammunition or recuperate part of the gas that accompanies the projectiles as they pass along the barrel defines a type of weapon whose main characteristic is its firing speed. The fact that the shoulder of the shooter receives less recoil energy because it is absorbed by the mechanisms of the weapon is another advantage.

The design of this type of shotguns is simple. The back segment consists of the stock, in the central part is the action and the front part consists of the barrel, which varies in length from 20" to 26" and usually incorporates a front sight and an inferior tube that acts as the magazine.

This type of semiautomatic shotgun has no standard capacity. Usually they are able to load up to three 12/70 mm shells, although the capacity can be increased. There are even standard models that have a bigger loading capacity. Many countries limit the amount of shells that can be held in the magazine in an effort to protect endangered species.

Different parts

The hand guard covers the stock and partially covers the action case and is usually made from the same wood or synthetic material as the stock. It allows the shooter to support the weapon with the left hand while aiming.

The stock helps to support the shotgun on the right shoulder. It usually ends in a rubber or synthetic butt plate that avoids slipping against the shooter's clothes. The lines of the weapon's design and the chasing on the stock help to grasp the weapon with the right hand.

The action case is located in the central part of the weapon and is the basic element of this type of shotgun. It is usually made of steel or aluminum, which is lighter, and incorporates various mechanisms that favor the movement of the shells and the firing. The trigger guard protects the trigger and a small device that allows manual re-loading of the tubular magazine. The action case usually incorporates a side lever for manual assembling and the breech through which the empty shell cases are ejected.

Semiautomatic fans

Semiautomatic weapons have a large and slowly growing band of enthusiasts. Semiautomatic shot-guns include some of the newest and best made firearms that are available on the market today. As well as their characteristic action, semiautomatic shotguns often in-corporate different types of muzzle chokes which adjust the pattern of the shot, enabling enthusiasts to practice different forms of hunting or sport shooting with the same weapon.

Semiautomatic shotguns are easy to aim, while the reduced recoil al-lows a rapid second shot if the first does not hit the target. However, different models of shotgun func-tion better or worse according to the make and weight of the shot used, and shooters must choose the shot with care to maintain the reliability of the weapon. In addi-tion, the more complex the weapon, the easier it is for it to be affected by the weather or by dirt.

The latest camouflage models help to conceal the hunter, especially when dressed in the same type of camouflage.

I : 102

left:
One weak point in shotgun designs is that they can be used to fire with any shell or charge. The ammunition must be carefully selected.

right:
Some of the newer semiautomatic models have an exterior finish that, together with the use of synthetic materials, allows their use in the most extreme weather conditions.

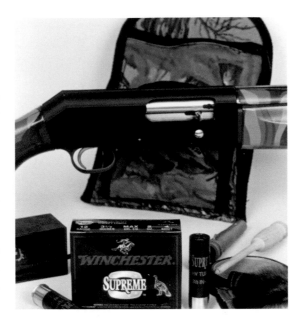

A wide variety of models

There are many different manufacturers, models, and designs of semiautomatic shotguns with a wide range of prices, making the choice of the correct weapon more difficult. It should be borne in mind when buying a semi-automatic shotgun that some weapons are better for certain types of hunting.

Italian models

Benelli is an Italian company that manufactures firearms in Urbino and also in Accokeek in the state of Maryland. From these two locations Benelli can supply the European and North American markets.

Innovation, technology and advanced design are some of the qualities that characterize their semiautomatic shotguns. They have a very wide range which is based on concepts like the Raffaello Crio that has received a cryogenic treatment, a special heat treatment of the barrel to obtain a suitable combination of hardness, elasticity and resistance. The Benelli inertia recoil design means that as the shot leaves the barrel the backwards energy on the weapon is reduced, the spring rebounds, throwing the bolt body backwards so that it unlocks the rotating bolt head, ejects the used shell and recocks the hammer. Then, the recoil spring returns the bolt assembly forwards and chambers the next shell, locking the rotating bold head.

Benelli's range also includes the Executive, which is available with fine engravings in the inferior part of the action case and the versatile Center that can use lead shot of 24 to 56 grams. The Super Black Eagle was the first semiautomatic shotgun to shoot the Super Magnum 89 mm shell. The Super 90 is mechanically simple

Because of the variety of possible clients, some models have very specific characteristic models, such as this SLUG-GLM which shoots shells loaded with heavy metal slugs.

and easy to maintain, while the Montefeltro shoots 20 gauge shells. The company also continues to produce some MI Super 90, including the Practical variant, which is adapted for dynamic shooting competitions.

Another great Italian company is Beretta, which has a commercial alliance with Benelli in the American market. The AL391 Urica model is provided with a valve located in the barrel, at the height of the front part of the trigger guard. Its function is to expel the gases that are not necessary to guarantee the operation of the automatic mechanism, a detail that provides much smoother shooting. Beretta also manufacture a total of eighteen different shotguns with various options of the AL391 Teknys, A391 3.5 Xtrema, 3901, ES 100 and 2001 FP models.

Fabarm is also an Italian company, with a very good reputation because their weapons incorporate technological changes such as the Tribore system which makes improvements to the bore which improve the placement of the shot. Its range is based on the Euro Lion and the Euro S which both fire Magnum shells. The Euro Lion includes three recoil and vibration absorption points in its action case that improve the sensation of the weapon for the shooter.

Some semiautomatic shotguns have a very high level of finish, including this Italian Franchi 48AL Field De Luxe.

American competitors

Mossberg has modernized its range with the semiautomatic 9500 Magnum series which includes eleven different models. The 24 and 26" variants, for example, are camouflaged entirely in Realtere Hardwoods HD Green and Mossy Oak New Break-Up. This range of weapons is characterized by their conceptual simplicity. They have a barrel with a muzzle that has a diameter of .775" as opposed to the traditional .731" muzzle thus improving the placement of the shot and reducing the recoil considerably. Another remarkable detail is that they are designed to shoot all types of shells including the 3½" Magnum. All the models in the series incorporate an optical fiber reference point for low-visibility conditions. Some models, such as the Grand Slam Turkey, can be equipped with an accessory that adheres to the muzzle and allows the more effective concentration of the birdshot, so that small targets such as a turkey's head are easily achieved by shooters with experience.

Winchester bases its offers on the Super X2 series, a design with thirteen different options. There are camouflaged models that are ideal for hunting, while others have a more traditional configuration with a synthetic stock and hand guard. Some models incorporate a mount for a telescopic sight that is fixed on the action case. The models of the Sporting concept are perfectly adapted for clay pigeon shooting. There are two Practical variants on the market for dynamic shooting competitions.

Remington have a wider range of models, including the 1100 type which has been manufactured for over four decades and which, in 2004, started to include .20 gauge options. The 1100 range includes the Synthetic FR/CL variant that has a redesigned stock and a scope mount fixed to the back part of the case, thus providing a shotgun that is perfectly adapted for hunting using rifle cartridges.

Remington also manufactures two semiautomatic models of the 11-87 Super Magnum type and two others of the 11-87 Premier range, which have an internal compensator that adapts them without problems to the shortest 2¾" shells. Browning has recently added the Gold Evolve model to its range. It has redesigned ergonomics to make it more comfortable. The tubular magazine is made of aluminum and its barrel is lightened to reduce weight to the minimum. It costs about one thousand five hundred euros.

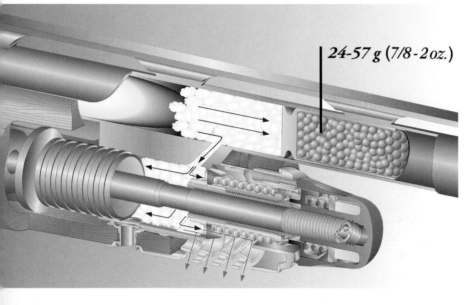

24-57 g (7/8 - 2 oz.)

This image shows how the automatic system works in shotguns such as this Beretta.

The automatic action of this range of shotguns allows rapid firing without losing sight of the animal that is in the sights.

Competitions vary in length, but in all the tension is maintained until the end of the shoot-off.

Clay pigeon shooting

Clay pigeon shooting

is a specialty in which the shooter must aim at and shoot down a small orange ceramic disc launched by machine in a random trajectory which must, however, be within a defined area. The shooter has to locate the flying target visually, aim the weapon, follow the trajectory of the disc and shoot it down with one small charge of birdshot. If he fails, he has a second opportunity almost immediately after the first shot. Clay pigeon shooting is not an easy discipline and requires much training. Competition shooting, whether in small or large clubs, or national or international tournaments, also requires, in addition to skill, the right weapon.

For fun and entertainment

Many hunters regularly practice another type of shooting when their hunting grounds are out of season, and the same shotguns they use for hunting can also be successfully used for clay pigeon shooting.

Olympic disciplines

Olympic clay pigeon shooting includes three categories: the pit or trap, the double trap and the skeet. Trap shooting is very popular in many European countries and numerous competitions of this type are organized. The competitions take place in shooting ranges that include a battery of fifteen launching machines that are half-buried so that they cannot be seen by the shooter.

The shooter normally gives a verbal sign, normally a single word such as "pull", to indicate that he is ready. The sound, captured by a microphone connected to special sensors, activates the launching of a disc that has a specific trajectory in function of the power and location of the machine. Therefore, the sportsman does not know beforehand what the trajectory of the target will be.

This type of shooting competition includes several series of twenty-five discs and the shooter can only use two shells per disc. In the Olympics and World Championships there are five series. The shooters that shoot down the largest number of discs go on to a final series or shoot-off to determine the winner.

Double trap

The double trap is a very recent variant of clay pigeon shooting, which was introduced in the 1996 Olympic Games in Atlanta, Georgia. The series consists of twenty-five doublets with fifty discs. Each launching order is followed by the launching of two discs that have to be shot down with only two shells.

There are three basic launching schemes, so the shooter does have an idea of the trajectory of the disc. The first scheme launches simultaneously from machines number seven and eight in the pit.

The second scheme launches from machines number eight and nine whereas the third scheme combines machines number seven and nine.

Olympic events involve a total of one hundred and fifty discs plus another fifty discs for the shoot-off. This expense, plus the high levels of skill and training required make it somewhat of a minority discipline.

The last Olympic clay pigeon shooting competition took place in Athens in the summer of 2004.

Skeet

Skeet is the most popular of the three Olympic disciplines and has been included in the modern Games almost since their beginning. Usually, series of twenty-five plates are shot, as in trap shooting, with international competitions including a total of one hundred twenty-five discs plus twenty-five for the shoot-off.

In skeet, the shooter has to shoot down one or two discs but only has one shell for each disc and loads one or two shells based on the number of discs to be launched. Skeet is the most mechanical discipline of the three, with a pattern that does not vary. The height and distance of the discs is always the same. In each series the shooters shoot from eight different positions which are covered by the teams according to the draw made at the beginning of the competition.

The best shooters

Clay pigeon shooting includes many levels of official and unofficial competitions, including international meetings which culminate every four years in the Olympic Games. The level of competition is very high. The Olympic trap shooting world record holder is the Italian, Giovanni Pellielo, who was the first to shoot down all 125 discs during the 1994 World Championship in Nicosia. The Italian team composed of Pellielo, Venturini and Tittarelli has the highest team score of 368 discs out of 375.

In the female competition, the Ukrainian, Victoria Chuyco shot down 74 out of 75 discs in a competition in Nicosia in 1998. The Chinese team obtained a score of 210 during the 1998 World Championship in Barcelona. In male skeet shooting, the world record holder is the German, Jan Henrik Heinrich, with a maximum score of 125.

Chinese competitors, like the Olympic champion pictured here, are at the forefront of the sport.

Only intense training can give competitors the necessary rapidity and accuracy for match shooting.

For safety, the shogun is broken and unloaded while the competitor awaits their turn to shoot.

I : 110

A general view of an Olympic-size clay
pigeon shooting range.

The Italian team composed of Falco, Benelli and Genga hold the world record for teams with a score of 368. In female skeet shooting, the Russian, Svetiana Demina, holds the world record with a maximum 75 score. The Russian team of Avetisian, Demina and Panarina obtained a score of 214 in 1999. In double trap shooting, the individual world record holder is the Austrian, Michael Diamond, with a score of 147 out of 150 and the team record is held by the Italian team formed by Di Spigno, Marini and Bernasconi with a score of 429. The female world record holder is Yafei Zhang from China, with a score of 115 made in 2000 and the team record is also held by the Chinese team, who scored 328 in a competition in Cairo in 2001.

Development of the competitions

Normally, competitors are divided into 4 categories: masculine, feminine, junior and veteran. Competitions are controlled by an official who ensures that the inscriptions and draws at the beginning of the competition follow the requisite regulations.

The objective

Clay pigeon shooting is highly skilled and needs intense training to achieve and maintain the high levels needed for all levels of competition. For important competitions, a training session is usually scheduled on the day previous to the meeting, usually in the same shooting range. The draw placing the participants in groups is usually made on the same day. Competition meets are subject to the regulations of the ISSF (International Shooting Sports Federation) or the FITASC (Federation Internationale de Tir Aux Armes Sportives de Chasse) in addition to the regulations of local and national organizations.

Everything is regulated, including the days allotted for training and competition, the make and color of the discs, the trophies, the manufacturer and model of the launching machines, accessories for the competitors and the prices of the inscription and discs.

Shoot-offs

After the main series are completed, there is a final round, known as the shoot-off, for the top six shooters in each category. These Olympic-type finals are held as long as there is a minimum participation of four competitors in each discipline.

The final shoot-offs is composed of twenty-five discs. If the scores are tied, a sudden-death tiebreak will be necessary, with the first competitor to miss being eliminated, except in trap shooting where ties for the first three positions are decided by an additional series of twenty-five shots. If the competition is still tied, a sudden-death shoot-off decides the winner.

I : 112

These are the machines which, hidden from the eye of the competitors, allow the automatic launching of the discs.

The Italians produce excellent weapons such as the Sport 6LM model which is ideal for clay pigeon shooting.

Specific rules

Clay pigeon shooting is regulated by what are known as the Special Technical Rules, which were drawn up the ISSF and contain details on all the most important aspects of the sport. The Rules state that any type of weapon with a gauge under 12 can be used, even semi-automatic weapons. Straps and the use of compensators are prohibited and the shooter's clothes cannot display advertisements. Shells cannot be longer than 70 mm, and the charge must be less than 24 grams (with a tolerance of + 0.5) and birdshot has to have a diameter of less than 2.5 mm. A Chief Range Officer is appointed to decide all technical and logistic aspects of the meeting.

There are many other regulations. For example, if a disc is broken on launching, the shooter can request a new launching. The barrels of the weapon must not be extended and the shooter's jacket must carry a reference point on which the stock is rested between shots.

The minimum elevation at which a disc is launched is one meter and the maximum four meters. The angle of launch of each machine is limited and based on a vertical reference and the maximum trajectory of each launch is fifty five meters in double trap and eighty in trap.

A long tradition

The United States have the largest number of participants in clay pigeon shooting. One of the most famous competitions to be held in the USA took place at the end of 1999 to commemorate the first centenary of the ATA (Amateur Trapshooting Association): seven thousand nine hundred and nine competitors met and shot almost five million discs at a range in Vandalia in Ohio.

The NSSA (National Skeet Shooting Association) has over two million members who shoot in more than a thousand shooting ranges located in every part of the USA. A sister organization is the NSCA (National Sporting Clays Association) who also promote competitions in which the shooters are placed in small booths and have to shoot down small discs launched in sequence by the launchers.

The color and size of each disc is different, imitating the flight of various birds, to simulate the feeling of hunting. This type of shooting is becoming increasingly popular.

The concentration needed to shoot down the small target is intense.

This type of weapon is popular among civil shooting fans worldwide because of its simplicity of use and easy acquisition.

Double barreled shotguns

Shotguns

are traditional firearms which date back centuries. In many countries, shotguns are an essential part of country life, and are widely used for hunting and for destroying sick livestock or shooting pests. While simple shotguns with one barrel are the most common, guns with two barrels, or even three have been a part of the gun world for many years. Double barreled shotguns can be divided into side-by-side guns – with the two barrels parallel to each other – and over-and-under shotguns – with one barrel superposed over the other –. Side-by-side shotguns have evolved functionally and aesthetically over the centuries and eventually gave rise to the over-and-under models, which are more elegant and make for easier aiming, since the shooter only sees only barrel. This kind of weapons is very useful in wildfowl hunting and an absolute necessity for clay pigeon shooters.

I : 116

Design changes

The last few centuries have seen small but significant changes in side-by-side shotguns, although the overall concept has remained remarkably unchanged. The first guns with side-by-side barrels had a firing mechanism consisting of two exterior triggers in front of the chambers. The shooter cocked them both individually, after which they could be fired in sequence. However, the first hammerless gun which had any success was the Anson

The Beretta DT10 over-and-under shotgun has an adjustable trigger.

Action mechanims

There is a general similarity in the basic components of side-by-side and over-and-under shotguns.

They basically consist of a set of two barrels united by an element near the chamber; an action to which the barrels are joined; a stock which is united with the action and an element that unites the barrels and action with the stock.

The action consists of the mechanisms which enable the barrels to be broken down to load and unload them and the trigger. Some models have twin triggers, one for each barrel, and dual actions.

In addition to uniting the different elements such as the barrels and stock, the action and its housing are often aesthetic elements of the gun, which traditionally are covered with fine chasing on the sideplates, especially in more expensive models. An English Purdey shotgun, for example, is an exclusive weapon which may cost over seventy thousand euros. Over-and-under models have different action designs. The Anson type places the actions in the interior of the weapon, adopting a less expensive and elaborate disposition than side-by-side designs.

and Deeley Hammerless Gun which received its patent in 1875. The success of the Anson and Deeley gun was almost entirely due to its design as a top lever opener which had greater safety of operation of the lock. This gun signaled the beginning of the development of the modern hammerless shotgun and the changes that have taken place since then have been relatively minor.

Both possibilities include an element that unites the barrels and fixes them onto the action to strengthen them and to allow a very robust weapon.

Characteristics

These types of shotguns can include a manual or automatic system for ejecting the spent shell cases. The automatic system has an extractor which automatically ejects the shell case to the rear.

This system is very popular in over-and-under models that are used in clay pigeon shooting. There are an increasing number of models which include chokes to modify and concentrate the pattern of the shot.

Mixed weapons have been designed based on the side-by-side models. They have a barrel that is adapted to classic shotgun shells – generally of the 12 gauge – and shells that can shoot metallic ammunition. With the dual option, different types of animals can be hunted without having to worry about the type of ammunition.

Better still, although not widely used, is the combination of two shotgun barrels with a rifled barrel in between them or two rifled barrels with a smooth bore barrel.

Craftsman can create concepts that are designed for specific customers and even combine two barrels adapted for shells of a different gauge.

Buying a shotgun

The wide and varied ranges of models that can be found in the catalogues of gun distributors make the choice of weapon difficult. The first consideration must be the use to which the gun will be put, as this, in large measure, helps decide whether a side-by-side or over-and-under shotgun is the best option.

The choice will also be influenced by aesthetic and functional criteria, but above all by the cost. With the price of this type of gun varying from three hundred to many thousands of euros, affordability must be the prime consideration for all but the most dedicated or wealthy gun lovers.

The Franchi range includes the Alcione model, which includes titanium in some of its metallic parts.

I : 118

European double barreled models

The catalogue of the German wholesaler, Frankonia (www.frankonia.de), gives a good idea of the large quantity of side-by-side and over-and-under shotguns that are manufactured in Europe. The first fifty pages show the different models and demonstrate the range of performance, price and manufacture that can be found.

Holland & Holland, a company that makes the finest side-by-side shotguns, is located in London. Their prices range from eighty six thousand to one hundred and eighty-eight thousand one hundred and fifty euros. This wide price range indicates the quality of the finish and the craftsmanship involved in the creation of these shotguns.

The different models of the Belgian company, FN, which produces the Faurieux range in a small factory specializing in shotguns located near the city of Herstal, are also of excellent quality. They also make custom made hand-crafted models to order.

Somewhat cheaper is the Merkel 60E side-by-side shotgun, with a price of around eight thousand five hundred euros. Its action and other metallic elements are hand engraved and models with gold chasing can be made to order.

All these shotguns are prohibitively expensive for the general user, although their craftsmanship and attention to detail makes them objects of envy to many gun lovers. However, for those who need simpler, less expensive double barreled models, the offer is also more than complete.

Italian shotguns

Italy, though it has never been a military superpower, has a justly famed reputation as a producer of firearms, especially shotguns and rifles. Today, Italian production of shotguns is largely grouped together in the "Consorzio Armaioli Bresciani" (CAB) which unites various companies, most of which are situated around Brescia, although some have their headquarters in Marcheno or Gardone Valtrompia.

The advantage of over-and-under shotguns is that they can incorporate a thread on the exterior of the barrel to fit a choke that modifies the shot pattern.

The action system of these over-and-under models enables both barrels to be cocked and broken down rapidly.

This commercial grouping represents the interests of companies such as Emilio Rizzini, Fair, Fabri, Falco, Fausto Stefano, Piotti F. Lli, Sabatti and Zanardini. Some of these companies specialize in very expensive shotguns for the wealthiest of clients, while others produce weapons that are notable for their originality. Piiotti, for example, continues to manufacture side-by-side models with external manual hammers while Zanardini has specialized in Express models.

They include details such as adjustable cheekpieces. Some of the series also offer single-shot weapons and hunting models such as the Extra, Extra Gold or Extra Super.

Franchi is another well-known name in the gun world. They produce the side-by-side Highlander model and the Veloce, Veloce Squire and Alcione over-and-under models. The Alcione SP is an attractive gun with a high- quality walnut stock and fine chasing which will satisfy all but the most demanding of shotgun enthusiasts.

Fabarm produces weapons of a similar type and quality. The over-and-under models include the Lux and Competition range with details such as the small holes located in the front part of the barrels to let the gas exhaust escape, reducing the muzzle flip and the firing recoil associated with the firing of a 12 gauge weapon.

In some over-and-under models, the action mechanism can be extracted rapidly for cleaning and lubrication.

As well as this consortium, there are other Italian gun manufacturers with a fine reputation. Perazzi produces over-and-under models of the MX2000, MX15, MX10 or MX8 series that are used for high-level clay pigeon shooting.

The famous Beretta company also produces hunting and sports models. The hunting range includes the side-by-side Silver Hawk 471, which is available in three different barrel lengths, and the Wing, Onyx, Ultralight and Pigeon over-and-under shotguns. The Pigeon has almost thirty different options of gauge, chasing and other details.

This type of weapons is ideal for sport shooting and hunting.

The range of sport shotguns includes models such as the 686 EX Trap Top Combo, which has interchangeable over-and-under barrels or a single top barrel, with an adjustable Monte Carlo stock with Memory System fitted to order.

The elegant 687 EELL Diamond Pigeon Sporting can fire 12,20, 28 and .410 ammuniton and is equipped with a streamlined stock, competition pistol grip and hand-finished floral motif engraving and checkering and has a single selective trigger and ventilated side ribs as standard.

The 682 Gold E X Trap has an exclusive International-style walnut stock with an interchangeable recoil pad and a non-selective single trigger.

The DT10 Trident Skeet has a dedicated skeet stock with a rounded recoil pad and a non-selective single trigger and is also available with a fully adjustable stock with Memory System.

In contrast, Antonio Zoli Corona is a shotgun craftsman. His over-and-under Kronos are a byword for perfection in the world of clay pigeon shooting.

Wildfowl hunting with over-and-under shotguns is becoming more popular because of the effectiveness of the weapons.

American shotguns

Various companies in the United States produce side-by-side and over-and-under shotguns, although in this area, unlike most types of weapons, European firms are carving out a large part of the American market for themselves.

Remington produces the 332 over-and-under shotgun, which is based on the legendary 32 model. Its barrels are made of an alloy of steel and chromium-molybdenum and are available in 26", 28" and 30" lengths according to the desired range. It has automatic ejectors and its metal surfaces are treated to improve their resistance to the weather or careless treatment.

Winchester has recently developed over-and-under shotguns that provide direct competition for the Remington models and match attractiveness with reliable working. Their models include the Energy Trap Adjustable Comb with an adjustable cheekpiece and trigger, the Energy Sporting with ported barrels, the Energy Sporting Adjustable Comp with 28" or 32" barrels and the Energy Trap, which has a stock that was especially designed for clay pigeon shooting and a Truglo optical fiber front sight.

Winchester also produces three over-and-under models in the Select series, including the Select Field which has the handling of a more expensive model at a reasonable price, and has an engraved receiver, and comes complete with a synthetic gun case for easy carrying.

Browning have recently produced a new over-and-under shotgun named the Cynergy. The design includes interchangeable butt plates to reduce recoil, chromed chambers to resist corrosion and a redesigned smoother trigger with a shorter pull. Currently, there are more than ten variants of the Cynergy. They complement the classic Browning Citori series, an over-and-under shotgun that combines elegance with classicism, technology with robustness and design with performance.

One of the latest models is the Citori Lightning, which is available in four different gauges and has been designed to have a light grip without losing the robustness and the details that are characteristic of this type of weapon. Browning also offers the BT99, a 12 gauge single-barreled shotgun, which has been manufactured since 1969 and is used for clay pigeon shooting.

The well-known American classic, the Winchester 1300, is an
excellent and robust weapon.

Pump action shotguns

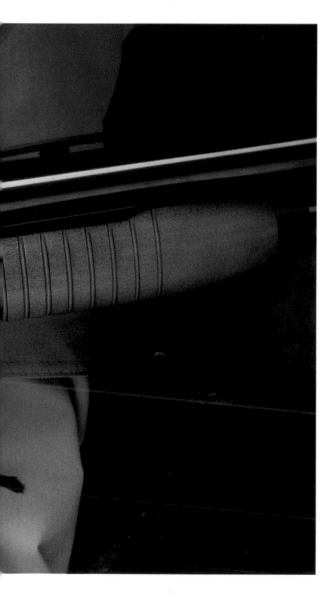

The simplicity

and, above all, the reliability of the pump action shotgun in all types of situations has given it an international reputation and boosted sales in recent times. The operation of these arms is totally manual. The shooter triggers a mechanism to introduce a shell in the chamber and to expel the empty shell case after firing the weapon. The name of pump action system accurately describes the forward and backward movement of the reloading actions. Although this system is slower than the semiautomatic and demands a certain adaptation to the concept and its dynamic qualities, it is fairly popular in the world of sport shooting, especially because these arms are used by the police and military.

I : 124

*Detail of the action case of
the Winchester 1300 Speed
Pump model, noted for its
robustness and long history.*

*Many pump action shotguns
have been renovated to
include accessories such
as auto illuminated aiming
systems.*

*Synthetic stocks and exterior
camouflage have allowed
the modernization of old
fashioned models.*

Action mechanism

Their simple use and easy maintenance make this type of shotguns extremely good for hunting. They are used, for example, in beats for hunting wild boar or in sport shooting disciplines like Action Shooting, a type of dynamic shooting that has handgun and long arms tests.

Advantages and disadvantages

American gun lovers, who are more accustomed to manual actions, know that a pump action shotgun is as good as a semiautomatic to bring down wildfowl such as geese or ducks or even fairly large animals, always assuming the shooter has sufficient training and experience and is using the right ammunition.

In general, the pump action shotgun has more advantages than disadvantages. They are very reliable, even in extreme climates or the worst weather. If a shell in the chamber fails — which is very rare with modern ammunition — it can be ejected and a new shell chambered rapidly without losing alignment with the prey.

Another advantage is their robustness, which is derived from their conception, without complex actions or elements that could provoke jamming. In addition to supporting the rough treatment that hunting implies, pump actions are also very versatile, with models that allow the barrel to be changed rapidly to accommodate different types of prey.

Pump action shotguns are, in general, reasonably priced, and they can be easily and quickly transformed to perform different tasks. The pump action shotgun can be complemented with accessories such as scopes, pistol grip stocks or folding stocks and even hand guards onto which a lantern can be fixed. In addition, the tubular magazine fixed under the barrel or the detachable magazines available with some models, usually have a capacity superior to five shells, bringing them within the restrictive legislation that is applied to hunters in many countries in an effort to conserve wildlife.

This kind of firepower is useful when different types of ammunition are used to bring down different kinds of prey. The pump action serves to eject the spent shell rapidly, allowing the hunter to load more suitable ammunition for each type of prey.

The manual design is a disadvantage. The pump action shotgun has a bad reputation among certain groups of hunters because it is thought to be slower than the semiautomatic shotgun, which is partly true. However, with practice, pump action shotguns can be just as effective as other, more expensive type of weapons.

It is true that pump actions shotguns generate greater recoil than semiautomatic shotguns, which partly absorb the energy that is released with each shot to load and eject the shells.

Manual action shotguns of all types are becoming more and more popular, and, as part of this trend, pump actions are being chosen by increasing numbers of users. This success is the direct consequence of the simple and robust conception of this kind of weapon.

The design of the pump action shotguns has altered little and is characterized by the relatively small number of mechanical parts. The most important elements are the barrel, the action case, the magazine, the stock and the trigger guards.

The barrel length can vary between fifty and seventy centimeters. The chamber size can also vary and is longer in the shotguns that are adapted to the 12/76 gauge ammunition, also known as Magnum. The 12/70 gauge is the most popular ammunition for this type of weapon.

The barrel is fixed to the upper front part of the action case, which is usually made of light steel or aluminum and includes a locking action and some elements of the firing system.

The magazine is usually a tube that is fixed to the barrel so that it fits below the barrel in front of the action case. The tube has a standard capacity of five or seven shells. They are retained by a spring until the movement of the action takes them to the chamber. The slide moves backwards to extract them from the tube and forwards load them.

Magazine feeding options are becoming more popular. The advantages are faster reloading and the variety in the type of ammunition used, but the disadvantage is the greater weight this system entails.

The stock usually has a butt plate in its back part to cushion the recoil. The element shared by the drive actions and the arc of the trigger guards protects the set trigger and prevents accidental firing.

Shotguns are used in some sport shooting disciplines that require dynamic, precise firing, as shown by this marksman with a pump action shotgun.

I : 126

Different models

American companies such as Remington, Winchester or Mossberg and Italian companies such as Fabarm, Benelli or Franchi include several pump action options in their catalogues. Each one has their own qualities and a design directed at a specific group of potential users.

Half a century of success

Pump action shotguns are often thought to be slower than other types of weapons, but experienced shooters, who can put three shells in the air at the same time go some way to refuting this myth.

Although it was conceived in 1950, the Remington 870 model is still one of the most popular designs. This model has a simple and effective safety mechanism – a drift pin located behind the set trigger – and its barrel can be changed very quickly.

The catalogue

The present catalogue includes options such as the Marine Magnum adapted to resist corrosion, the Super Magnum Turkey Camo that is available with 26" or 28" barrels or the Express type that has about fifteen different options on the same base. They also offer models with two options of barrel type and shells.

The 1300 Winchester model is very successful. It is a design that has about twenty different options in barrel length, general finish and technical details.

Mossberg offers, in addition to the less expensive Maverick, the 500, 590 and 835 models, which exist in a wide range of finishes, designs and options. The 835 models are ideal for hunting because they are available with long barrels to use all the potential of the Magnum shells. They can even have rifled barrels that are adapted for shooting bullets.

Italian models

The various Fabarm pump action shotguns have similar qualities. In some markets they are marketed together with Heckler & Koch weapons. Their SDASS and FP6 models are adapted for different needs. The FP6 excels due to the finish of the action case and the ergonomic hand guards.

Benelli includes in its catalogue various models of the M3 Super 90 series that can be adapted to shoot manually or in semiautomatic mode. A few years ago they introduced the advanced Nova concept that includes camouflaged options and is available with Slug barrels adapted for shooting heavy metal slugs.

Franchi continues to produce the SPAS 15, which has a magazine with a capacity for six shells as well as the classic PA 7 and PA 8 models.

Pump action shotguns are suitable hunting weapons.

Camouflaged models are very popular among hunters in many countries.

Detachable models fit nicely into a small gun case.

The range of models and options of telescopic sights is wide, and includes this scope for a precision rifle.

Sights and scopes

Shooting is a sport

in which maximum accuracy is vital, whether in target shooting or hunting. In search of this objective, marksmen and hunters usually increase the accuracy of their long arms with accessories that improve their aim, such as sights and scopes. There is an infinity of types designed to fit the needs of each group of potential users.

Pentax is a Japanese manufacturer with a line of interesting products.

On target

Sights have evolved enormously over the centuries. Today, there are models with up to 36x magnification, lenses of the highest quality which give an extremely clear image, and even night sights for shooting in the dark.

Traditional designs

This is the 4-12x50 AO viewfinder made by the Japanese company, Nikon, which has excellent magnification and luminosity.

Telescopic sights have a basic configuration, with no outstanding differences between models. The manufacturers offer classic telescopic sights, systems which incorporate a red dot that is projected onto the target, holographic systems and even optronic devices that can intensify residual light.

The classic telescopic sights consist of a metal tube with lenses fitted to the front and back, which enable the shooter to magnify the image – the target or prey – that has been acquired. The sights include mechanisms which can regulate for width and height. The whole system is usually sealed to protect it from rain, dust and humidity.

The more recent classic telescopic sights include a reticle that is illuminated at night and can include reference points in its central part.

One of the top-of-the-range American products is this Mark 4 3-9X36 MRT M1 made by Leupold.

Quicker focusing

Telescopic sights with red dots such as the Tasco Red Dot Scopes, which offer ruggedness and long eye relief, are more modern. They are smaller than the classic models and the traditional reticle has been replaced by one shining dot that is generated by a special LED. These models do not magnify the image a lot because they are designed for situations in which the shooter must aim quickly, almost instinctively.

Bushnell offer solid products at a reasonable price.

Holographic telescopic sights include a screen on which a reference is electronically projected. The field of view is usually circular to be able to focus better on the target zone. This conception avoids the tube effect that is generated in the two previous types of telescopic sights.

The optronic viewfinder is a design that can be used in bad light or in the dark. These models incorporate an advanced electronic system that catches the residual light generated by stars and other light sources and increases

Hunters and shooters usually use telescopic sights to increase accuracy and to identify their targets.

it thousands of times, thereby allowing a more or less clear observation of the target zone. There are also models that use an older technology based on infrared rays which are invisible to the human eye.

Optronic telescopic sights are normally not used by sport shooters and their use in hunting has been restricted in certain countries. The big exception is the United States, where their use is permitted.

Mounting the scope

Powerful rifles, like this Armalite Ar-30 which fires .338 Lapua Magnum caliber ammunition require telescopic sights that are adapted to resist the recoil generated by so much power.

The various concepts and designs of carbines, rifles or shotguns have different systems for mounting scopes. They are usually fixed to the action case for stability and to avoid the pressures generated by the shot, although some models that are designed for faster alignment with the target can be connected to the barrels.

Scopes are normally fixed on the mounts included in the gun by the manufacturer or custom-maker. Different types of mounts are used for permanent scopes and detachable scopes.

Telescopic sights that are fixed onto the barrels are anchored with two circular rings that can be located anywhere on the barrel. This kind of viewfinder is better for rapid shooting as opposed to precision modes and is mainly used for action shooting.

Fixing night sights is more difficult. However, night sights like the Trijicion self-luminous iron sight can provide shooters with five times more night fire accuracy with the same speed as instinctive shooting, which has given Trijicon a reputation for extremely reliable night sights. Trijicon Bright and Tough night sights are the sights of choice for many of the biggest manufacturers.

A wide range of models

Although the world market is huge and recent years have seen the eruption of various cheaply priced models, especially from the emerging economic superpowers of Asia, the United States, Japan and Germany are still the leaders in this field, due mainly to the quality of their products.

American producers have the benefit of a home market composed of millions of gun lovers. Japan has established a good reputation in optical products since World War Two, while one only has to think of the long list of German camera companies to understand their excellence in the field of optics, although recent economic developments have meant that their lens, never cheap, have become less competitive than the products of other countries.

American models

Leupold is a very well-known company which has been producing models that are popular among sport shooters and hunters for over a century. Their models unite excellent manufacture, very high quality and a reasonable price and have been adopted by the police and military, which is always a guarantee of quality. Interestingly, the company also produces binoculars and accessories for bird-watchers and other nature lovers.

The top of range is the Mark 4 model. It is available in the fixed M1 version with 10x or 16x variants, and in the M3 version which has 6x or 10x options. They are completely waterproof – the units are submerged in a tank with water at 120° to verify this quality – and they are available with adaptable turrets that enable the shooter to vary the impact point rapidly and effectively.

There are about ten different options in reticles. The most popular are the Duplex, Mil-Dot, Crosshair and those that include modern illumination systems for use in bad light.

Recent models such as the VariX-I 3-9x50mm, VariX-II 4-12x50mm and Rifleman 3-9x50mm have optics with a 50 mm opening allowing a clear vision of the target and are especially adapted for the hunting market. The series that include the Rifleman 3-9x50mm are moderately priced, making them available to all kinds of users, including sport shooters.

To fix the telescopic sights to the rifles it is necessary to use mounts with the adequate diameter, height and robustness.

Bushnell is another large American manufacturer. Their range includes the recent Elite 3200 series, and the Holosight holographic viewfinder with advanced holographic technology which helps you zero in on the target as soon as you raise your weapon, and which projects an illuminated crosshair some 50 yards in front of your weapon without projecting any forward light.

The series includes a model that has 320 hours of battery power, is fogproof, waterproof and shockproof. Models such as the Trophy 1.75-4x32mm have a camouflage covering.

Burris offers the Euro Diamond, Signature Select or Black Diamond Titanium series, which are well-known for their image brightness, resolution and clarity. Their latest range includes models such as the Short Mag that is adapted for powerful arms or the novel Xtreme Tactical which has a tube of great resistance and adjustable turrets.

Other companies that offer this type of products are Weaver, with models like the Grand Slam 6-20x40 mm, Simmons, with the ProHunter series with diverse types of auto illuminated and normal reticles, and Springfield Armory which manufactures the 4-14x56 mm 3rd Generation Government Model 7.62 that includes an inner level to ensure that the shooters position is stable and a reticle with reference points that facilitate aiming with 7.62 Mach ammunition at a distance of up to 1,000 meters.

Simplicity

Japanese products are normally cheaper and less complex, although both their quality and their price has been increasing.

Tasco produces the Titan, World Class or Pronghorn ranges. The TG104050DS 10-40x is adapted for long distance precision shooting, while the T312x52NA viewfinder is very popular among some groups of hunters and the MAG type includes four designs that can be adapted for weapons shooting .22 LR caliber ammuntion.

Nikon is a world-famous name and their products in this field do justice to their tradition. Their present range is based on concepts such as the economic Buckmasters, the more elaborate Monarch, the multipurpose Prostaff and the excellent Tactical and Titanium, which is available in 3.3-10x44 AO or 5-16.5x44 AO options.

However, Nikon's two star products are the 3-9x40 Silver Shadow with a silver-plated exterior finish which has proved to be a great success and the 3-9x40 mm Team Realtree, which has a camouflaged finish and is nitrogen sealed for 100% waterproofing.

The use of red dot telescopic sights in arms such as shotguns allows greater agility while aiming.

European products

European products tend to be of excellent quality but considerably more expensive than their Japanese or American competitors.

One of the companies that enjoys an international reputation is the German firm Schmidt & Bender which has been manufacturing telescopic sights for over fifty years.

The 1.5-6x42 multipurpose model, which is available with an illuminated reticle, the 10x42 model that is ideal for big game hunting and the 3-12x50 model which can be fitted with several types of reticle sell well to those for whom quality is more important than price.

Zeiss is another famous German name. Their Diatal and Diavari series include options such as the resistant 6x42 mm MC or the powerful ZM/Z 3-12x56 mm MC. When talking about German companies, we should also include Docter Optic, which sells more than a dozen models, some with an illuminated reticle.

Swarovski is considered by many as the company that makes the best telescopic sights. Their high prices are reflected by the clarity of vision and their extraordinary capacity to absorb light. Models like the PH2.5-10x56 or the PH3-112x50 of the PLEXN series cost about one thousand five hundred euros.

The Swedish company Aimpoint has had great success with their compact red dot telescopic sights. Their models, with the Comp-M2 model as the top of range, are waterproof and shockproof and are designed to exclude any possibility of parallax errors.

Red dot telescopic sights, like this Aimpoint 7000, allow hunters to aim rapidly at close quarters.

Cartridges can be loaded manually
or with a magazine, although not all
ammunition is suitable for both.

Ammunition

The chapters of this book

have reviewed a large variety of types and models of long arms. The world-wide market offers all kinds of variants, capacities or uses and there are many different sport or hunting specialties in which long arms can be used. Each one of those specialties requires a type of ammunition that is adapted to the needs of the shooter. Even within a specific speciality there are different options because the needs and objectives of the different users vary. For this reason, the market offers all types of ammunition. There are different sizes, benefits and capacities because each type of projectile will have a different ballistic efficiency depending on the cartridge used.

I : 138

The origin of the ammunition is also important.

Different types of ammunition are produced by arms manufacturers all over the world, mainly for domestic markets. However, some companies have managed to establish an international reputation due to the quality of their products or the range of ammunition that they supply.

The high accuracy arms used in 300 meter shooting competitions require Mach cartridges that are generally of the .308 Winchester caliber.

Recent legislation in some countries has prohibited the use of lead shot, from January 2008, forcing the manufacturers to use substitute materials, although in many countries this prohibition is already in force.

The reason is that lead is highly toxic and lead shot has led to the

These cartridges of the 28 caliber have been designed for clay pigeon shooting.

death of many animals that ingest it, above all birds and wild fowl. Manufacturers today are turning to ammunition made of steel, tungsten-iron, tungsten-nickel-iron, bismuth, and even tungsten polymer.

Rifle cartridges

Independently of their actions, rifles normally use metallic cartridges, although there are some gun enthusiasts who still prefer muzzle loaders, charging their guns manually as did their forefathers: powder, projectile, cleaning rod and primer.

The metallic cartridge includes powder lodged in a metal container that is crowned by the projectile that closes the superior opening and exists in hundreds of different calibers.

Handgun ammunition

Some rifles are chambered to shoot traditional pistol and revolver cartridges. Many manufacturers follow this fashion and adapt their models to ammunition like the .38 Special, .357 Magnum or 9x19 mm Parabellum. The ballistic qualities of these three types of ammunition are poor, even when long barrels

are used to give greater stability to the bullets. This means they are more suitable for informal shooting than for hunting although they can bring down small prey at a short distance.

Ammunition such as the .44 Magnum or .45 Long Colt can also be shot with some handguns, generally revolvers, but it is more powerful and better suited for hunting. There are also models that are adapted to the .45 ACP or the variant, the .45 Winchester Magnum.

The .22 Long Rifle

In spite of the diversity of the market, the .22 Long Rifle ammunition remains the most-widely sold.

All types of carbines and some rifles use this ammunition because it is very accurate at fifty or one hundred meters. It is one of the most widespread types of ammunition among shooters practicing Olympic disciplines. It is also popular among informal shooters due to the fact that is low price allows enthusiasts to shoot for longer. Its bullet, whose weight oscillates between 2 and 2.6 grams, has a limited capacity for hunting, although a rabbit or hare can always be brought down with it.

When fired with semiautomatic weapons, they can bring down small pests or rodents, especially because there are now high speed options that have a remarkable kinetic energy.

The .22 Winchester Magnum is derived from the .22 Long Rifle. It has a bigger powder charge and better benefits. In certain areas it is even used to hunt small, light animals.

Identifying a cartridge

The general designation of ammunition depends on its origin. In the USA, Canada, the United Kingdom, Australia, New Zealand and other English-speaking countries, the denominations refer to a diameter measured in inches (one inch = 25.3995 mm). For example, to identify ammunition with a diameter of 0.416 of an inch, the zero is omitted and the ammunition is known as .416 plus the name of the manufacturer or the inventor or developer. Two examples are the .275 Rigby and .425 Richards.

Another designation combines the diameter with the charge for which it was conceived. In the .30-30 Winchester, the designation is accompanied by the name of the manufacturer.

The diameter and year of manufacture can also be combined: the .30-06 Springfield, for example, refers to a cartridge designed in the year 1906.

Some cartridges are the result of adapting an already existing cartridge case. For example, the .25-06 Remington is a transformation of the .30-06 cartridge whereas the 7-08 Remington is based on the .308 Winchester.

In Europe, ammunition is usually designated using the metric system and normally includes the caliber of the projectile and the length of the cartridge case. Examples are the 7.62x39 mm or 7x57 mm ammunition.

Muzzle-loaded long arms also benefit from the appearance of new projectiles such as this expanding bullet.

The South African company, PMP, produces a wide range of rifle cartridges adapted to different needs.

Sport shooting includes new disciplines which demand new types of ammunition such as this .50 caliber designed by McMillan.

Recently words have been added to the name to identify various qualities such as high power (Magnum, Express) or great accuracy (Match).

Ammunition for different uses

The range at which a type of ammunition can be effective or the type of animal that is hunted determines, among other factors, the choice of the most suitable ammunition. For example, for hunting at short to medium distances, the popular .270 Winchester, with suitable stopping power when it shoots bullets of 150 grains, the well-known .280 Remington, also known as the 7mm Express, or the versatile .30-06 Springfield, which has variants that shoot bullets ranging from 55 to 220 grains, are all ideal.

The .300 Winchester Magnum, with its excellent stopping power, and the 7 mm Remington Magnum, are more powerful. Even more so are the .375 Holland & Holland Magnum, widely used for hunting in India or Africa, the .416 Rigby which can shoot down an elephant, and the powerful .458 Winchester Magnum which can include projectiles of up to 510 grains.

The most powerful ammunition is the .600 Nitro or .700 Nitro, with bullets of up to 1,000 grains. The .222 and .223 Remington (5.56x45 mm) which is suitable for informal shooting sessions, the 6 mm PPC or 6 mm BR which are very accurate and the versatile .308 Winchester (7.62x51 mm) are cartridges which are widely used among hunters.

The .308 Winchester is used for competition shooting at distances of 300 meters, for hunting and high precision shooting, using a different projectile for each type of shooting.

The large manufacturers

The largest ammunition manufacturers are all American, and include Cor-Bon, CCI-Speer, Black Hills, Federal and Winchester.

Winchester's 2004 catalogue offers various new hunting options. The Accubond CT type allows shooting at great distances and has great expansive power to big down big game such as elk or bear.

The Ballistic Silvertip range has great stopping capacity, whereas the hollow tip Failsafe also has excellent expansive power on impact. Winchester has enlarged its range with new concepts such as the 25 WSSM (Winchester Super Short Magnum), which is a compact cartridge with great accuracy and performance.

The more recent products introduced by Federal include the Premium V-Shock series, which fires very accurate AccuBond bullets, and the Premium V-Shok series, which includes new high-speed .17 caliber ammunition that has superb accuracy.

The CCI-Speer range has been enlarged to include new concepts and charges within their Nitrex line, of which the Grand Slam type is the best known. It ranges from the small .243 Winchester to the powerful .458 Winchester Magnum with a solid tungsten bullet.

Other choices

The most important European manufacturers of ammunition are Norma of Sweden, Lapua of Finland and RWS, which is a German company.

 Norma produces some thirty cartridges for rifles, which range from the .22-250 Remington to the .458 Winchester Magnum. Other well-known options are the Jacktmach, which is adapted for precision shooting and the Trophy XP that is adapted to obtain the necessary deformation for bringing down prey with a single shot.

Lapua, a company that belongs to the Nordic Ammunition Company (NAMMO) group, produces precision ammunition. The .308 Winchester, .338 Lapua Magnum and others can used with Scenar, Lock Base or Mega type bullets.

Scenar bullets can be used to obtain groupings of ten impacts within a circle of 12 mm at three hundred meters; Lock Base bullets are characterized by their high velocity and Mega bullets are more suited to hunting. Other well-known companies are the South African, Pretoria Metal Pressing (PMP), Woodleigh of Australia and Hirtenberger of Germany, which uses the accurate Nosler and Sierra bullets.

In the United States, the .50 Browning, with which elk can be brought down at a distance of over one kilometer is becoming very popular.

The cartridge belt is a useful accessory for hunters because it allows many cartridges to be carried.

Shotgun ammunition

Although there are some over-and-under shotguns that include a rifled barrel adapted to shoot rifle ammunition, shotguns normally shoot shells. These usually include a metallic detonator cap, which closes the chamber and receives the shotgun primer in its centre, and a plastic case which contains the propellant and the projectiles – shot or slugs.

Different gauges

The caliber of shotguns is determined by the gauge number, which refers to the number of solid spheres of a diameter which is equal to the inside diameter of the barrel which can be made from a pound of lead (489 grams). Thus, a 10 gauge shotgun signifies that the interior diameter is equal to that of a sphere made from one tenth of a pound of lead. Today, the most popular

Winchester Supreme ammunition is one of the most recent innovations of this famous company.

Lately, new cartridges have been developed to satisfy the needs of specific groups of gun lovers.

gauges are 12 and 20, although there are many others. some gauges such as the .420 caliber are still measured in inches due to historical reason.semi metal shells have a metal and a plastic section, which can be paper or cardboard in older models. Their designation refers to the number of pellets that can be manufactured from a pound of lead (489 grams).

The 12 gauge is the most popular option. The normal version measures about 70 mm and the extended variant 76 mm (3 inches) and is designated as Magnum. The 12/70 gauge usually has a small-shot charge that oscillates between 30 and 36 grams while the Magnum has charges that weigh between 40 and 50 grams. There are longer and shorter options but these are rarely used by hunters and shooting enthusiasts.

Ten gauge shells are used in duck and geese hunting. The 16 gauge is gradually losing popularity. The 20 gauge is becoming more popular in its normal and Magnum versions and the 28 or 32 gauges are ideal for shooting small wildfowl without damaging the piece excessively. There are even .410 shells that are normally shot with a metallic charge.

Shot size

Shot is usually designated as either birdshot or buckshot. Although there is no precise definition, it is usually accepted that buckshot has a diameter greater than 0.20 inches, while birdshot is smaller. The pellets that make up the shot are designated by numbers which range from 12 to 2 for birdshot and 4 to 1 and then 0, 00 ("double ought"), and even 000 ("triple ought"). Slugs, which are single projectiles with a larger diameter used to hunt wild boars or deer are designated from 000 to 0 for the smallest ones. Some shells, like the French "chevrolines", even include smaller balls but in greater quantity.

For hunting small wildfowl such as quail, small charges of fine pellets are normally used. As the size and vitality of the prey increases, heavier charges and bigger pellets are needed. For hunting rabbits and hares, the 6 shell is used while the 00 shell is more useful for hunting foxes.

Various models and manufacturers

These type of shells can also be charged with bullets although the smooth barrels of the shotguns will not provide great accuracy. Among the more popular is the Brenneke type, which is grooved for better stability. However, it is not accurate beyond eighty to one hundred meters.

There are several types of bullets for shotguns , including armor-piercing bullets. The French Sauvestre has a design similar to the projectiles used by modern armored cars. It was created by an association between high technology and innovation and the Sauvestre FIP bullet with a carried internal arrow is both bimetallic and leadfree. It is extremely accurate due to its original design and has almost total stopping power which is due to its penetration and hydrodynamic cavitation.

The cost of a box of twenty-five 12 gauge shells is about five euros, with more expensive variations depending on the type and manufacturer.

In spite of their low cost, there are more elaborate types that come in a box of five, such as the Super Brenneke Sabot bullets which cost between 19 euros if they are normal or 22 euros when the charge is Magnum.

Winchester has recently introduced the Super Target shells with lengths of 2 ¾ and 3 inches for clay pigeon shooting. The Italian company Fiochi has increased its range with the Low Recoil Slug and Golden Pheasant types, whereas the Czech company Sellier & Bellot offers several options in its 12/70 Mark III, Lord, Crown, Fortune or Extra ranges.

Cross-sections of some of the most powerful ammunition.

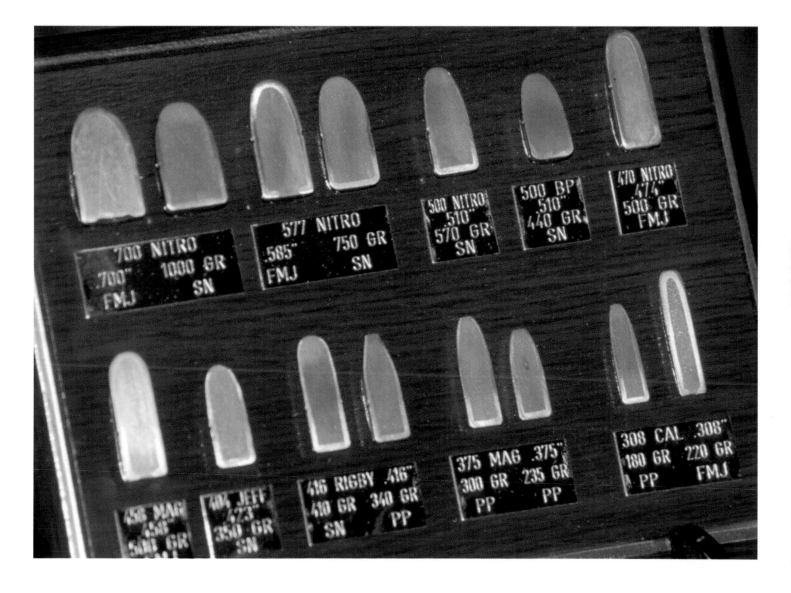

Photo credits